Client/Ser
& Beyond:
Strategies for
the 21st Century

Lisa-Ann L. Barnes
David J. Shimberg

Foreword by Neil Evans

To join a Prentice Hall PTR Internet
mailing list, point to:

http://www.prenhall.com/mail_lists/

Prentice Hall PTR
Upper Saddle River, NJ 07458

Library of Congress Cataloging-in-Publication Data

Barnes, Lisa-Ann L.
    Client/server & beyond : strategies for the 21st century /
Lisa-Ann L. Barnes, David J. Shimberg.
      p. cm.
    Includes bibliographical references and index.
    ISBN 0-13-532516-1 (pbk. : alk. paper)
    1. Client/server programming.   I. Shimberg, David J. II. Title.
QA76.9.C55B38   1997
004'.36--dc21   96-51030
                               CIP

Editorial/production supervision: *Patti Guerrieri*
Cover director: *Jerry Votta*
Cover designer: *John Fitzgerald*
Manufacturing buyer: *Alexis R. Heydt*
Marketing Manager: *Dan Rush*
Acquisitions editor: *Mark L. Taub*
Editorial assistant: *Tara Ruggiero*

©1997 by Prentice Hall PTR
Prentice-Hall, Inc.
A Simon & Schuster Company
Upper Saddle River, NJ 07458

The publisher offers discounts on this book when ordered in bulk quantities. For more information, contact: Corporate Sales Department, Prentice Hall PTR, One Lake Street, Upper Saddle River, NJ 07458, Phone: 800-382-3419, Fax: 201-236-7141, e-mail: corpsales@prenhall.com

Printed in the United States of America
10 9 8 7 6 5 4 3 2 1

ISBN   0-13-532516-1

Prentice-Hall International (UK) Limited, *London*
Prentice-Hall of Australia Pty. Limited, *Sydney*
Prentice-Hall Canada Inc., *Toronto*
Prentice-Hall Hispanoamericana, S.A., *Mexico*
Prentice-Hall of India Private Limited, *New Delhi*
Prentice-Hall of Japan, Inc., *Tokyo*
Simon & Schuster Asia Pte. Ltd., *Singapore*
Editora Prentice-Hall do Brasil, Ltda., *Rio de Janeiro*

CONTENTS

PREFACE

The journey of a client/server project team is not much different from that of Jim Lovell aboard Apollo 13. The team may see the destination but be forced to turn back due to unforeseen events. Although the development team's lives may not hang in the balance as the project is turned around, their jobs certainly are at risk.

This book seeks to be a source of practical wisdom for those people who have key roles in the success or failure of a client/server project:

- Chief Information Officer (CIO)
- Project manager
- Developer (analyst, designer, programmer, tester)

The book provides these three groups of people practical solutions and strategies to be used during the process of developing and delivering client/server applications. This book does not require detailed technical knowledge or deep project management experience in order to be beneficial. The only prerequisites for readers include:

- A knowledge of the general software development process and terminology

- An understanding of client/server complexities and issues
- Some hands-on experience developing applications

THE BOOK'S ORGANIZATION

Information is organized and presented in a top-down approach, based on a general development process. Success factors and strategies are discussed at the relevant level of the organization and stages of the development process.

Although each section of the book is geared towards a specific audience, we encourage you to read the entire book. By doing so, you will gain an awareness of the challenges faced by other members of the Information Technology (IT) organization. Each group will also develop an understanding of how the other roles in the organization are performed.

The rest of this section describes the book's organization.

Part 1: The Big Picture

We first address the tasks that must be done by the CIO to prepare the entire IT organization for success with client/server development.

- *Chapter 1: Client/Server Challenges and Realities* provides a big picture perspective on the current state of client/server development.
- *Chapter 2: The Success Factors* defines the general influences on client/server success.
- *Chapter 3: Setting the Stage for Success* discusses the specific strategies and solutions that must be implemented by the CIO.

Part 2: Preparing for Project Success

In this section, we look at the success strategies specific to an individual project. A detailed view is provided for the project manager, who is responsible for the "how" and "what." The project manager receives valuable information on preparing for individual projects.

- *Chapter 4: Building the Best Team* defines the roles necessary for client/server projects and discusses an approach for staffing.
- *Chapter 5: Following the Right Process* presents methodology selection and usage strategies.
- *Chapter 6: Establishing the Development Infrastructure* provides techniques and strategies for building the necessary environment for client/server development.
- *Chapter 7: Managing Chaos* addresses project management techniques and critical concerns.
- *Chapter 8: Knowing the End-Result* describes how to define and scope the project to increase the chance for success.

Part 3: Client/Server Success Techniques

The third section of the book focuses on solutions to common client/server challenges. We provide the developer with proven tips and techniques for each stage of the client/server development process.

- *Chapter 9: Defining the Details* focuses on the requirements-gathering process.
- *Chapter 10: Avoiding Analysis-Paralysis* describes analysis techniques for client/server development.
- *Chapter 11: Designing for Success* provides success strategies

and solutions for the design and prototyping stage of the development process.

■ *Chapter 12: Putting It All Together* addresses the concerns of the final stages of development—construction, testing, and implementation.

■ *Chapter 13: Creating the Architecture* addresses the specific issues related to the client/server architecture developing.

Part 4: Future Directions and Challenges

We conclude this book by looking at the future of the industry and how emerging trends and technologies will impact the IT professional.

This section also contains a list of suggested readings and the glossary.

HOW TO USE THIS BOOK

This book's purpose is to identify, describe, and suggest solutions for success in client/server development. This book will not provide you with all the answers—it will prompt you to think.

As you read our solutions and strategies, reflect on your organization.

■ What is your role within client/server development efforts?

■ What are you and your teams doing well?

■ What suggestions of ours have you successfully implemented already?

■ What can you do to improve? (Don't disregard any ideas because "that won't work here.")

■ What must be changed to "make it work?"

■ What is the basic premise of the suggestion and how can you implement it?

You want to succeed at your client/server efforts; if not, you wouldn't be reading this book. If you are an executive, you must develop strategies to provide these critical items. You must then support your project managers by providing the necessary budgets for training, tools, and other resources.

If you are the project manager, you must implement the strategies on your projects. Demand the best people and make sure your team is spending time on skills improvement activities. Allow time for the inevitable learning curve associated with new processes and tools.

If you are the developer, the strategies are implemented as a direct result of your actions. Use the process and tools defined for your project. Read industry publications and attend training to learn about technological changes; keep upgrading your skills.

Although the book deals with client/server issues, the issues that are addressed here affect every project, regardless of the technology being implemented. As today's technology matures and new technologies emerge, the basic success strategies related to people, process, technology, and tools will still be with us.

We believe that technology is an enabler, not a driver. The technology will change, but the challenge of delivering quality applications on time and within budget will not disappear.

ABOUT THE AUTHORS

L isa-Ann Lingner Barnes is the president and founder of Knowledge Transfer Associates, Inc., a software development consulting and training company. Lisa-Ann is a recognized expert in systems development methodologies, speaks at industry conferences, and has been quoted in industry publications such as *The Wall Street Journal, ComputerWorld,* and *PCWeek.*

Lisa-Ann's background includes strategic planning, software design and development, project management, and methodology implementation. She has experience in all aspects of the client/server development and implementation process. She combines these experiences to help Fortune 500 companies in the United States, Canada, and Europe have an easier transition to client/server solutions. She works with their Chief Information Officers, application development managers, and project managers to:

- Assess readiness for client/server efforts
- Create organizational structures and project teams
- Implement and customize methodologies
- Establish a development infrastructure
- Scope and estimate projects
- Determine skill requirements and training needs
- Develop and deliver technical training

In addition to her experience as a consultant, Lisa-Ann has significant experience developing and delivering training. She has developed over 20 courses in Information Technology topics, and has delivered training to over 2,000 students.

As a consultant, her recent clients include Equity Group Investments, Amoco Oil, and Andersen Consulting. Prior to starting Knowledge Transfer Associates, Lisa-Ann was a member of Andersen Consulting's FOUNDATION team. She also served as the Chief Methodologist for a software firm, rated by the Gartner Group as one of the leading consulting companies in client/server development techniques; the firm was acquired by LBMS.

David J. Shimberg is a Principal of SalesWorks, Inc., a Sales Force Automation consultancy with responsibilities focused on client requirements for technical direction, process analysis, and related issues. David has a unique combination of strategic vision and leading edge technology skills.

David's background includes executive-level strategic planning, information systems design, project management, and implementation of client/server solutions within the Fortune 500 environment.

In the role of vice-president of Information Services for Chrysler Systems, he directed the transformation of all internal and customer-based systems from legacy to client/server. While engaged by Chrysler, he also shared responsibilities as National Sales Manager with four other key executives.

In addition to Chrysler, he has provided consulting to Andersen Consulting, the United Nations, the Michael Jordan Foundation, Lotus Development Corp., Equity Group Investments, Kemper Financial and a long list of other satisfied clients.

David's recent accomplishments include a cover story in *DBMS Magazine* and a feature article in *Data Management Review*. David serves as a member of the Board of Governors of the Information Management Technology Resource Center

(ITRC). ITRC is a nationally recognized non-profit organization that offers technical assistance to charitable organizations. He is a chairman of DCI's Field & Sales Force Automation conferences with a special focus on Tools and Technology.

ACKNOWLEDGMENTS

We would like to thank the following people without whose help this book would not have been completed!

- Our friends and families for their patience, understanding, motivating, and listening.
- George Pavel for editing, polishing, and making it read like one voice.
- Paul Vinopal and Jeff Lyons for reading our drafts and giving us feedback on how to make them interesting, readable, and clear.
- HRH for introducing us to each other.

Lisa-Ann L. Barnes & David Shimberg
September 1996

FOREWORD

The successful development and implementation of leading edge business systems is a balance of art and science. As my career evolved from that of programmer to CIO, I was always challenged to find meaningful sources of strategic wisdom and practical systems' science. My mission critical business systems projects left little room for "trial and error" as a viable technology strategy.

The role of information systems as a strategic competitive tool is ever expanding. Technology management teams are under intense pressure to make decisions at the right time and anticipate the expected results. Whether the project at hand is client/server based or web-server based, there is often a sense that, strategically, technology managers are pioneers seeking clarity in uncharted waters.

The authors of this text have provided a clear roadmap for Information Technology (IT) managers and staff. They have fully recognized the challenges and pitfalls that frequently stand in the way of successful technology deployment in today's business world.

From the early days at Microsoft through more than 10 years of dynamic, high pressured growth, the critical role of structure, discipline, and strategic vision never diminished. As we began our efforts to migrate Microsoft's mid-range technology to a client/server platform, we carefully analyzed risk and developed a phased plan to move forward. Pioneers have seldom had a road-map to follow. Projects did not always proceed as planned, but each effort constantly added to our insights, so we were more effective with our next initiatives.

Today, after rising to the position of Microsoft's first CIO, I have retired from the intensity of managing Microsoft's internal business systems. However, I clearly recognize that my success was based on skilled and committed staff, discipline, and structure. I have now moved on to new challenges as the Executive Director of the NorthWest Center for Emerging Technologies. I have responsibilities for raising more than $10,000,000 from the National Science Foundation, Microsoft, Boeing, and other parties interested in developing curriculum and direction for students who seek to understand and participate in Information Technology careers.

Our program is committed to building a curriculum where students can gain a practical set of technical and procedural skills, which meet the needs of the business community. We currently focus our efforts on tactical skills which PC, LAN, and Internet jobs demand. The strategic issues presented throughout this text support our goals for the future.

Strategic vision within the IT environment has generally been realized on-the-job. There have been few practical resources that IT professionals could depend on to gain insight into the challenges that ever-changing technology presents. Whether we are building a client/server sales management system to track Microsoft's world-wide product sales or deploying an Internet Web site, clear, concise strategic resources are critical. Technology is a moving target and those who are most effective learn early in the game to develop strategies they can depend on. Having a clear foundation will help IT apply concepts to new technologies. IT will be better able to recognize that Internet technology is, in some sense, "back to the future," with browser/server tools being used as just new buzzwords for a client/server implementation.

Lisa-Ann and David have combined years of experience and knowledge into a well thought out guide to strategic information systems success. This book clearly offers its readers a roadmap to move forward into the 21st Century with effective and competitive information systems. Whether your needs focus on traditional client/server development or technologies such as those that surround the Internet, the underlying concept presented throughout this text remains constant.

Neil Evans
Executive Director
NWCET

PART 1

THE BIG PICTURE

CHAPTER 1

CLIENT/SERVER CHALLENGES AND REALITIES

Change:
To cause to be different

Challenge:
A test of one's abilities or resources in a demanding
but stimulating undertaking

Reality:
The quality or state of being actual or true

C hange happens. Change happens with an exceptionally rapid pace in the Information Technology (IT) industry. When change in technology occurs, it has far-reaching consequences. Client/server technology is a change that impacts all aspects of our business systems. Change as dramatic as client/server technology also causes business expectations to be reset in all areas. The expectation of client/server technology is that it is faster, easier, and more flexible to develop and deliver. It is not just a coincidence that corporations today expect significantly more value from their technology investments, in a shorter time frame, than during earlier eras. What is expected, however, is not always based on fact, and is therefore not always realistic!

Today technology is distributed to desktops, laptops, network servers, wide area networks, and global web servers. More importantly, information driven through IT systems has gained recognition as a primary corporate asset, a necessity to building and maintaining a competitive advantage. The client/server environment is still relatively new. Very quickly, though, we have discovered that the glass walls no longer protect the IT domain. The structure, methodologies, securities, skills, development process, and tools—virtually every aspect of what worked before—no longer translate into an effective IT organization for client/server technology.

On the personnel side, the Chief Information Officer (CIO) has been pushed to take a visible place as a senior business executive first and a technician second. The high turnover rate at the CIO position is generally the result of a failure to quickly and effectively align business goals with the ability of IT to deliver. IT no longer has the "luxury" to gather business needs and show up two years later with the solution. How does the CIO stay on top while the chaos caused by today's client/server environment settles down? In addition to the technology chaos, the business environment surrounding IT is continually evolving. How can the CIO effectively balance the organization's business realities with technology changes?

With client/server technology, the IT project manager is confronted with new project management challenges that absorb staff time and force old skills and strategies into obsolescence. How does a project manager strategically respond to the pressures that surround the need for successful implementation of client/server technology? Where to start? How to succeed? The project manager must learn to manage expectations, educate the customer on how to clearly express customer needs, and expose the development team to these customer needs and business processes. The customer's perception is that Graphical User Interface (GUI) software can be developed and implemented within a six to nine month span. Right or wrong, this drives project plans and budgets.

The members of the development team are not immune to the swirling cloud of change, either. Most mainframe developers are aware that not every one of them will be interested in, or capable of, making the transition to a GUI, iterative development, relational database, open system environment. Experience shows that between fifty and seventy percent of existing mainframe developers will make an effective migration to client/server. How do they make the transition? How long will it take? What skills are still valuable? What new techniques must be learned?

This is the reality facing today's IT organization. Client/server technology is here to stay. The business community demands higher quality applications—faster and cheaper. The CIO, project manager, and developers must make the transition to this new business and technical environment. Success in migrating to today's environment is dependent upon IT:

■ Recognizing their new role in the organization
■ Aligning themselves with the business
■ Assessing their level of readiness

IT'S NEW ROLE

The role of IT is being forced to change by the rapid, drastic changes in the business environment. IT must understand this new business environment and its new role in order to be a part of the picture. Businesses are getting "leaner and meaner." They are downsizing, right-sizing, and reorganizing. In order to be more competitive, businesses are forced to assess the way they operate. Costs are being reviewed—IT can no longer submit a request for funds and resources and not be questioned on the amount. IT is now considered an investment opportunity, not just a cost of doing business. Options for providing technology solutions used to be limited—build it in-house. Now the options include outside development, outsourcing, and purchasing packaged solutions. IT is being run as a profit center, not a cost center.

As a profit center, IT must provide quality customer service. Business units will no longer accept mandates to use technology given to them. If they are not happy with the service or solutions they receive from IT, they will go outside to get what they need. Therefore, IT must manage their customer relationships over time and during projects. The psychology, or "the politics," of managing customers in a client/server implementation is as large a factor for project success as the tools, staff, process, and platforms. We cannot emphasize enough the impact of the re-distribution of power between IT and the business units and the control that the customer has in today's information environment. Critical to IT's success is the recognition of its role as a service provider to the business units.

Example—Insurance Company

The Information Systems department was not reacting favorably to their customers' requests for access to the critical business data stored on the mainframe. Customers were forced to submit requests for reports and then wait several weeks for the reports to be developed and the results delivered.

After missing several key business opportunities, the business unit that had the greatest need for the data hired a team of five people, installed PCs and a network, created a data warehouse, and provided the other business units with access to the data they needed.

Many IT organizations have built an interaction style that reflects the personality of its leadership and to some degree its "glass house." The perception that IT is too complicated to be understood by the average person must be shattered. If IT is viewed by its customers as intimidating and not user-friendly, it will be difficult to provide quality customer service. To break down this perception, you should develop and execute an internal marketing plan prior to the start of the migration to client/server. This plan focuses on surveying the business community while developing the mechanisms to improve communications, perceptions, and understanding. This plan also communicates to the rest of the organization: IT's role, their customers, and what services they will provide. Prior to finalizing this plan, a "customer satisfaction survey" should be completed, at least informally. It is an eye-opening experience. The survey should include questions such as:

- How is IT perceived by the business community?
- Does IT respond to their problems in an effective, timely manner?
- Does IT understand the problems facing their customers?
- Does IT communicate clearly with the business managers?
- Does IT listen to the business managers?
- Does IT encourage communication with the business community?
- In what areas can IT improve?

This survey will provide the IT organization with the information necessary to execute its new role as service provider in a business-focused, client/server environment.

ALIGNING IT WITH THE BUSINESS

Client/server technology is aligned with IT's new role. It is hard to say which came first, the technology or the role. Regardless, they are both here to stay. Client/server technology is also aligned with the new relationship between the business community and the IT organization. The modularity, granularity, and distributed nature of client/server technology reflects the departmentalized business model. Increasingly, the business unit is responsible for their own development budget. They drive the project definition, scoping, and timing process for IT initiatives. If they don't get what they need when they need it, they will create their own technology solutions.

The speed of change to the departmentalized business model and client/server technology has been incredible. Power has shifted from the mainframe and manual processes to the desktop and associated technologies. How well has your IT department been able to support this transition? Ask yourself:

- Have you been able to provide desktop solutions? Quick access to data?
- Are your business users dependent on IT to provide them with their data, or have you given them the tools they need?
- Have they obtained those tools without your help?

The answers to these questions will tell you how attuned IT is to the business's needs.

To gain this perspective, spend a day interviewing some of the newer staff in your accounting department. Focus on the number of ad-hoc spreadsheets, forms, and documents that are interwoven into the daily workflow of the staff. Now, find an "old-timer" who is willing to talk to an IT team member (sometimes a challenging task). Engage in a conversation about the good old days in the accounting department, pre-1990. Talk about columnar pads, month-end close, accounting runs, and the volumes of reports. So much of the work was done manually.

Meeting rapidly changing business needs is the historical Achilles Heel of the IT world. Managers are so focused on putting out fires related to technological change, project deadlines, staff turnover, staff skills development, budget challenges, and resource limitations that they often have little time to pay attention to the business that surrounds them. To be successful today, you must look outside IT first—identify customer needs, trends, directions and still somehow maintain a course through the constant pressures of technology changes. Success is very much dependent on IT management's ability to take an objective view of itself and the leverage that it can bring to any business decision-making process.

As you prepare for client/server projects, it is important to have a clear sense of the corporate vision and direction. Is the business in a volatile growth environment? Is your organization in an acquisitions mode, a growth mode, or a downsizing mode?

The management of today's IT group, driven by client/server projects, requires the skills of a politician, psychologist, business expert, and technocrat. Information Technology no longer exists as an island unto itself. Long gone is the day when users wait in line with their card decks, hoping that IT will run their jobs. The customer is empowered with expectations of more responsive applications, applications whose navigation is user-dependent (not menu-driven), flexible, and fast. Solutions must evolve in a rapid manner, supporting data integration and distributed access anywhere and anytime. Management is given the unenviable tasks of keeping the customer satisfied, conquering new technology platforms, and moving the corporate information systems onto the information superhighway. And this all must be done while being aligned with the changes in the business environment!

Example—Holding Company

The company's IT group was not aligned with the business needs or with technology changes. The group could not answer the question: "Who is your customer?" They did not know if they served internal departments, related companies, or affiliated companies. They also did not know the priority that one customer's needs had over another's. They were also severely out of touch with recent technological advances. The existing technology was "legacy"—business applications that are dependent on software development tools, hardware, and operating environments that are no longer supported by the product's vendor. Their legacy applications included core, mission-critical business systems, such as financial systems, payroll, and accounting.

In some cases, the legacy technology could no longer be modified to meet current or future needs; source code to certain applications no longer existed, having been lost or destroyed. Approximately 80 percent of the IT team's time was spent on support and maintenance tasks. There was very little development work occurring, neither integration of packages nor development of custom applications.

This organization had not been focused on the business or technology in many years; people in the organization were not ready for client/server development. Upper management was evaluating outsourcing options as an alternative to moving the existing group forward.

ASSESSING READINESS FOR CLIENT/SERVER

Once IT understands its role and is aware of how it must be aligned with the business, the high-level work is done. It is then time to prepare the IT organization for success. The first step is to assess your readiness to move forward with client/server technology. What is your level of the focus and understanding required to successfully buy, build, and implement client/server technology? In many cases, this assessment should be completed by an outside resource—it can be difficult to remain objective and complete an honest assessment of strengths and weaknesses. Even IT shops that have been early adopters of client/server technology fall into bad habits. Open up your organization to an outside perspective so that you can honestly identify areas of strength and weakness.

The assessment looks at the four primary success factors for transition to any new technology: people, process, technology, and tools. These four factors are discussed in more detail in *Chapter 2: The Success Factors*. The assessment provides a statement of your current level, or as-is situation. It should also provide you with a goal, or to-be situation. Then you must develop strategies to move you from one level to the next.

- When looking at the level of readiness for your people, focus on their skills and structure.
- What functions does your IT organization provide?
- How are your development teams structured? Client/ server teams are most effective when they are limited in size from 8 to 12 team members. This is a far cry from the 50 to 100 team members engaged in a mainframe development effort.
- How will you structure teams using the client/server model?
- How do you support communication with the business community?
- What tools are used to assist the team in communications such as groupware, version control, process management, etc.?

The weakest link in IT's ability to respond to the changing demands of client/server is the availability of skilled, highly capable technical resources. Success cannot occur without recognizing the changes that will impact IT's resources. IT's success will be dependent on a core group of highly capable, experienced technicians and business analysts. *Chapter 3: Setting the Stage for Success* and *Chapter 4: Building the Best Team* provide strategies for organizing your IT organization and development teams.

Examine your development methodology:

- Do you follow a standard development process?
- Will it support client/server development efforts?
- Are the developers trained in using the methodology?

When moving to client/server technology, a methodology becomes an invaluable guideline and source of knowledge. *Chapter 5: Following the Right Process* provides strategies for selecting and implementing a methodology.

Assess your current technology direction and infrastructure:

■ Is there a known, stated direction?

■ What is the current state of integrated applications and data?

■ Do you know where all your applications and data are residing? If you have chaos, how will you retain control?

The new IT infrastructure must not only support the distribution of data, but it must also recognize the need to centralize and redistribute desktop data sets. Business managers must be educated on the value of integrated, shared, and secured data sets. Because IT has been slow to respond, and technology and business have been running on their own super-highway, the politics of taking away data that moved to the desktop without structure, plan, or standards becomes an IT cultural challenge. Through it all, the technology direction must keep a perspective on the corporate direction. Strategies for setting technology direction are provided in *Chapter 3: Setting the Stage for Success*.

Assess your development tools:

■ What is the level of automation you have in the development process? What tools are being used?

■ Are all the developers sufficiently trained on the tools?

■ What standards are in place?

■ Are you building GUI applications that "look and feel" the same as published standards, or do they look the same as CICS screens?

In *Chapter 6: Establishing the Development Infrastructure*, we describe the development tools and standards necessary to succeed with client/server technology.

SUMMARY

Moving to client/server technology is full of challenges and opportunities that must be managed head-on. There are few shortcuts that improve IT's ability to develop, deploy, support, and maintain client/server technology. To succeed in today's business and technical environment, IT must:

- Recognize their new role in the organization
- Align themselves with the business
- Assess their level of readiness

A recent study of client/server projects conveys an image similar to the evolution of our children[1] We all start out excited about our newborn. Later, when the projects reach the "testing" phase (otherwise known as adolescence), we wonder whether they will ever evolve into functional, independent adults or if they will be lifelong projects. Unfortunately, less than half of client/server projects delivered today actually become solutions that businesses can use. Throughout this book, we will provide you with proven techniques to better that ratio.

[1]Gartner Group, white paper, "Client/Server: A Study of Usage and Benefits."

CHAPTER 2

THE SUCCESS FACTORS

Success:
The achievement of something desired, planned, or attempted

Factor:
One that actively contributes to an accomplishment, result,
or process

Today, you cannot open an industry trade magazine without reading another story about another client/server project failure. Studies still show that between 50 and 80 percent of client/server projects fail! These projects are either never completed or the application is deemed unusable by the business end-users. So how does the Chief Information Officer (CIO) explain this to the business community and upper management? How does the CIO justify the move to client/server in the first place? Should project managers slated with the first client/server implementations kiss their careers good-bye?

Many of the challenges faced by the Information Technology (IT) team are generic to client/server implementations. The solutions are also project-independent. If these general challenges are met successfully, then the complexities of specific projects can be isolated and addressed. To succeed in today's business and technology environment, the CIO and project managers must migrate to client/server, but in a logical, thorough manner, which addresses the general concerns that are inherent to all client/server projects.

People who have already failed at a client/server project by diving directly in will be the first to say, "If only we had done x, y, and z before we started the project." They wish they had staffed the project differently, or dedicated more time to training on new techniques and tools, or used a different development process, or clarified the technology direction. Instead of doing those things prior to the project's start, they either missed major project deadlines or didn't finish the application. These people have uncovered the factors critical to the successful implementation of any new technology, especially client/server:

- People
- Process
- Technology
- Tools

Our experience shows that almost all the problems encountered during client/server implementations can be traced to improper preparation of people, process, technology, or tools. To succeed with any technology migration, these four areas must be the primary focus. Understanding the technology and buying the fanciest tools are not a guarantee of success if the people and processes are ignored. And if the people are trained and organized properly but not given direction or the necessary tools, you will not be successful, either. All four factors impact success and must be treated with equal importance.

This chapter defines each of the four implementation success factors and provides some overall success strategies for client/server development. Remaining chapters discuss the factors and success strategies in more detail. Although the four factors are discussed individually, these implementation factors are tightly integrated and cannot realistically be analyzed apart from one another. For example, you cannot develop strategies to upgrade your staff's skills without knowing your technical direction or the tools to be used for client/server development.

PEOPLE

"People" refers to the staffing, roles, team structure, and skill building that provide the best possible team for a client/server project. "People" also refers to the development of strategies that address staffing and skill-building needs that will prepare staff for the roles and responsibilities required for client/server projects.

The best team consists of prepared people with the required skills to fill specific, discrete, and effective roles. It is an undisputed fact that client/server development requires different skills and roles than earlier forms of development. Have you identified those new roles? What is being done to prepare people for client/server development? Will new skills be built, bought, or borrowed?

Options for building the best team do exist for the CIO and project manager. These options must be evaluated in terms of cost and benefit, as well as the intangibles such as morale and reputation. Too many times, more attention is given to the short-term bottom line than the long-term results. For example, training costs are frequently allocated to the first project that requires new skills. A more realistic approach is to allocate the costs across all projects that will use the skills gained. Another approach with a long-term view is to establish a standard training budget for each employee. It is not unrealistic to spend two thousand dollars per employee per year for technical skills development. That training cost can be compared to the costs associated with replacing outdated employees with new, more expensive employees, or with temporary contract workers.

Staffing strategies for building the best team include:

- Updating existing people with new skills
- New people hired with solid client/server development experience
- Consultants (make sure they transfer their knowledge to the project team!)
- A mixture of existing people, newly hired people, and consultants

Chapter 4: Building the Best Team defines the client/server staffing process and roles in more detail. When reading that chapter, remember that strategies need to be developed to transition people from one set of skills and responsibilities to a new set. These strategies include:

- Change Management—Communicate rationale, expectations, and future actions
- Staffing—Identify the roles and team structure required

■ Skill Building—Identify, develop, and deliver the training necessary to build the skills required

PROCESS

"Process" refers to the selection and use of a standard and appropriate methodology that provides clear definition of the roles to be staffed, tasks to be completed, and deliverables to be created during the development cycle of an application.

Within many organizations, people cringe at the "m" word. "We don't need a methodology. We're too small. Methodologies are too big. It will take away our creativity. We've never used one before. We have experienced people." Methodologies provide guidelines and structure, which if taken to extremes *can* cause problems. But when used properly, methodologies provide a roadmap and identify the sights to see on the way.

Think of a methodology as a recipe. Instead of making pie, you're making a business application. When you first try a new concoction, you stick closely to the recipe. You use the full two tablespoons of butter, you carefully measure the flour and sugar, and you let it bake for the complete hour. You may taste the mixture and add a little cinnamon or nutmeg, but you stay true to the directions. There are things you'll keep the next time, but you refine the recipe with time. The same thing can be said of your first client/server project—you follow the directions very closely. You're not sure exactly where the trouble spots may be, what new techniques and tasks you must do, and what the best timings are. Those types of "seasonings" you refine over time.

The next time you try the recipe, you may choose the low-fat option and replace the butter with margarine or cream cheese. You also add a lot more cinnamon. As your experience with client/server development increases, you identify tasks and deliverables you don't need, modifications to timings, and other changes. For example, you may determine that the information recorded on two distinct deliverables is best done during one step and on a combined deliverable. You also find yourself referring to the directions less and less.

Over the years, IT organizations have developed expertise in mainframe development. Some organizations have also developed expertise in the methodologies being used. As a result, people feel they don't need a methodology because they know what they're doing. With client/server, the desired end result is new and different. A structure, or recipe, is needed to get to that end result. Don't start a client/server project without something in place. It may not be the easiest recipe to prepare, or the option lowest in fat, but use something! Refine the approach over time! Just as you wouldn't try to make a new dessert without using a recipe, don't try to build a client/server application without a methodology.

The development process and methodology requirements are defined in more detail in *Chapter 5: Following the Right Process.* Just as with the "people" factor of client/server implementation, a well-defined migration approach needs to be developed. The approach must address:

■ Development approach and methodology selection

■ Implementation and customization (including training)

■ Ongoing ownership and maintenance (including quality assurance programs)

TECHNOLOGY

"Technology" refers to the development and use of a technology strategy in order to help select the components of the deployment environment. The deployment environment is the technical environment in which the client/server applications will run. (The development environment is addressed in the

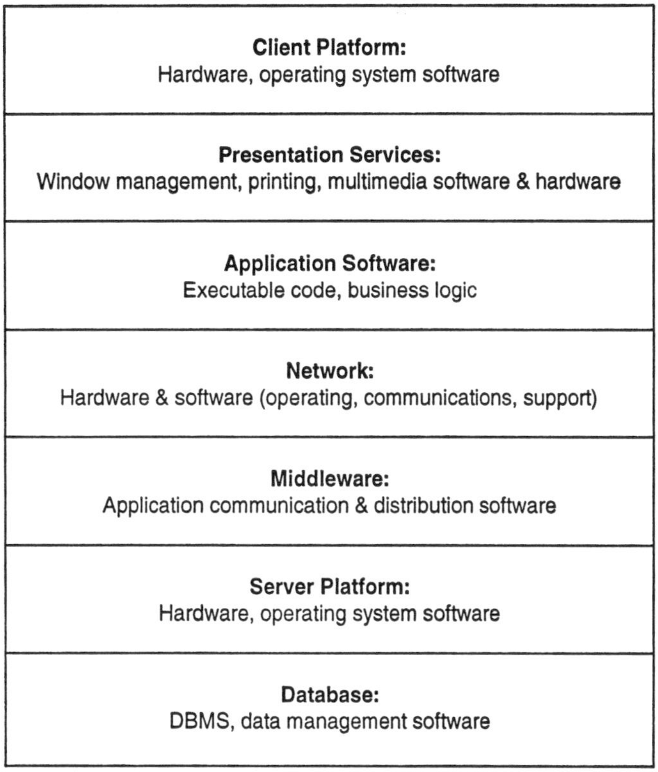

FIGURE 2-1.   Deployment environment.

Tools section later in this chapter.) The technology strategy must address all aspects of the deployment environment, as defined in Figure 2-1.

A technology strategy is essential for long-term success with client/server. Today, there are an almost unlimited number of combinations of technology available in which an application can be deployed. This openness is one of the basic strengths of client/server technology; it is also one of its biggest challenges. To take advantage of the technical strengths of client/server, a strategy must be in place. This strategy includes the basic parameters and fundamental decisions about the technologies to be used and their implementation. These parameters and decisions are embodied in an organization's technical direction. The technical direction is influenced by the business direction and needs of the company, as well as the direction of the hardware/software industry.

When an IT organization does not have a technology strategy, the customers (end-users) and support teams can be pummeled with a different deployment environment for each application. It is very easy for each project to select its own technical environment. They build the application then "throw it over the wall" to the maintenance and support teams to deal with. This creates chaos and corporate waste. For example, if systems are to be integrated, lack of a strategy causes costly rework. Lack of direction may also lead to technical dead-ends. To avoid this, each project must fit into an overall strategy.

This does not mean that an organization should have one and only one standard deployment environment. What is appropriate for the sales force may not be appropriate for the accounting department. One of the appealing factors of client/server applications is the openness of the architecture. This provides flexibility in matching the technical environment to the needs of the customer. The organization must, however, have a big picture of how all the various applications will be deployed and integrated.

Then, each project identifies the technology components that provide the necessary functionality, but *within* the parameters established by the overall technology strategy. The detailed requirements for the technical environment are gathered as part of each project.

Chapter 3: Setting the Stage for Success identifies the components of the technology strategy in more detail. When reading that chapter, remember that strategies are needed to transition from one technical environment to another. The strategies include:

■ Developing an inventory of existing deployment environments

- Evaluating the current state of the industry and trends
- Migrating from one environment to another

TOOLS

"Tools" refers to the creation and use of a development environment, or infrastructure. The infrastructure consists of all the items needed for the development of an application, from operating systems to communications to development standards. Basically, the infrastructure consists of all the tools, standards, services, and templates used by the development team to deliver client/server applications. The components of the development infrastructure are very similar to those of the deployment environment, as illustrated in Figure 2–1. The major area of difference is the application software layer. For the development environment, the application software layer consists of development tools, testing tools, development guidelines, object classes, libraries, standards, and templates. There are also standards, guidelines, and tools for other layers, such as the database and network layers.

Infrastructures were less formal during the mainframe era. The development team was experienced and did not require formal guidelines and standards. Due to the mainframe's centralized nature, the architecture was simpler and had fewer layers. Also, the infrastructure was imposed by the hardware environment, and in many cases, the components of the infrastructure came with the hardware. With client/server development, the infrastructure is critical to the success of the project. There are also many choices for each layer, especially the application software layer. The establishment of a basic infrastructure provides cross-project leverage and skill-building for the entire IT organization. Why should each project spend valuable time researching and selecting development tools and standards? Those tasks should be completed once and the results made available to each project team. This allows each project to build on the accomplishments of prior projects.

The technology strategy provides the starting point for determining the specific pieces of the infrastructure. The decisions made regarding the deployment environment will provide the first level of evaluation criteria for the development environment.

■ Will tool X develop code compatible with the stated deployment environment for a specific end-user group?

■ Will it develop code compatible with all the deployment environments described by the technology strategy?

■ What user interfaces must be supported by standards?

■ What testing tools are compatible with what development tools?

■ What libraries are available for what tools?

■ How do these development components fit into the environment for the development team?

■ Are they compatible with the mail system and office software products?

■ What are the hardware requirements and how are they impacted by the technology strategy?

The amount of centralization depends on the size of the IT development organization and the number of new client/ server applications that will be developed over the next three years. If the development organization is large (30 people or greater) and over 30 percent of the new projects will be client/ server, the infrastructure should be formalized and centralized. In these cases, the infrastructure is developed and maintained by a central team, which dictates the standard components to be used by all projects. This central team may even provide technical support for these products. This team may also provide internal consulting services, such as quality assurance, usability reviews, and tools training.

In smaller organizations, the infrastructure can be developed and maintained by a small part-time team of people whose participation rotates on a quarterly basis. This greatly increases cross-project communication, leverage, and skill building. Chances are, this type of team already exists, but is not recognized.

Regardless of the IT organization's size, it is more important to develop the infrastructure than to finalize how it will be managed. Just as with a development process, start with something and refine as time passes. Ideally, the infrastructure is established prior to the start of any client/server development. In reality, it is built project-by-project. At the very minimum, the infrastructure can be specific to a project, using informal input from team members of other projects.

The specific components of the infrastructure are defined in detail in *Chapter 6: Establishing the Development Infrastructure*. When reading that chapter, try to answer these key questions for your organization:

■ What components should you standardize? How will you decide?

■ What components do you have in place? What level of expertise exists with each?

■ How will the development of the infrastructure affect your development teams? What training will be needed?

SUMMARY

The critical factors of client/server implementation are people, process, technology, and tools. The success ratio for client/server is higher if the CIO and project manager recognize these factors and develop the necessary success strategies. These strategies include:

- Building the best team
- Following the right process
- Selecting the appropriate technology
- Establishing the development environment

CHAPTER 3

SETTING THE STAGE FOR SUCCESS

Prepare:
To make ready beforehand for a specific purpose

Success:
The achievement of something desired, planned, or attempted

T here is an old Sicilian phrase that should be memorized by every person in management: "The fish rots at the head." In Sicily, if a fish is served without its head, it won't be eaten—it is certainly rotten. This phrase aptly summarizes every management failure and describes every management success. Basically, this phrase states that the success or failure of every effort is dependent on the capabilities of the head management. If there is solid direction and management from the top of the organization, then the rest of the organization has a chance for greatness. If the top of the organization fails in its responsibilities, the rest of the organization can only be mediocre, at best. This phrase applies to the Information Technology (IT) organization as well as to any other organization.

In most companies, the Chief Information Officer (CIO) is the "head of the fish" for all technology initiatives. These initiatives can be broken into two basic categories—infrastructure and application implementation. Infrastructure initiatives include the development and support of the organization's technical backbone: computer networks, desktop and departmental systems, communication systems (voicemail, e-mail), and telecommunications networks. Infrastructure initiatives also include the ongoing support and operations of the deployment environments used by the company. Application implementation initiatives relate to the application of technology to a business problem, either through the development of a custom solution or through the implementation of a pre-packaged solution. Therefore, the CIO is ultimately responsible for the overall success of each and every application development effort.

Chapter 2: The Success Factors defined the factors that are critical to client/server success. Ensuring that the proper people, process, technology, and tools are in place is the responsibility of the CIO. For client/server projects to have a fighting chance at success, the CIO must ensure that the overall organization is geared for success. This is accomplished both through actions and through attitudes. The CIO influences success by setting priorities, establishing strong business community relationships, providing budgets for resources, training, and tools, and fostering a team-focused culture.

Once the IT organization has assessed its level of readiness (as discussed in *Chapter 1: Client/Server Challenges and Realities*), the CIO must build the specific strategies to prepare for client/server development. These strategies must be communicated to the IT organization for the project managers and developers to execute. This chapter provides the CIO with strategies for ensuring that projects will succeed and the fish will not rot.

The CIO is responsible for:

- Tying technology solutions to business needs
- Structuring the Information Technology organization
- Creating the technology strategy

TYING TECHNOLOGY SOLUTIONS TO BUSINESS NEEDS

Currently, a CIO can expect to remain in his or her position for 14 to 16 months. This high turnover rate is related, somewhat, to the CIO's failure to tie technology to the business. The CIO must set a clear direction and purpose for the IT organization. This direction and purpose must be framed in business terminology, not technical terminology. Too often, the CIO comes in to the position, assesses the state of technology, and demands more resources to "bring things up-to-date." The CIO says that these resources are needed to go client/server, but can't articulate what benefits the business will gain from the investment. As the tenure duration indicates, the rest of the organization cannot accept this lack of business understanding.

If the CIO, the head of the fish, cannot articulate what benefits the application of technology will bring to the business, how can the rest of the IT team? How will the team know what projects are top priority? How will the team determine each project's value to the business? How can the team have a customer-focus if they only view technology as important? If the technology changes, how will each individual view his or her value to the team?

In order for the members of the IT team to answer these questions, the CIO must craft a clear and meaningful statement of purpose. This purpose must provide a clear and complete:

- Definition of the customers
- Statement of how they are to be served
- Description of the services to be offered to these customers
- Statement of how these services support the overall business purpose of the company

Note that this statement is not technology-focused, it is customer-focused. This statement of purpose provides the team with an understanding of its role in the overall business's purpose.

Many times, we walk onto the IT floor, see the company's mission statement on the wall, and then see the IT group's mission statement next to it. Too many times, there is no connection between the two statements. When you ask team members, from project managers to developers, how their job supports the overall business, they can't tell you. They can tell you about the benefits of one programming language over another, though. This situation is unacceptable. Business needs must drive technology solutions. IT must be closely aligned with current and future business needs.

STRUCTURING THE ORGANIZATION

Once the customers and services are defined, the CIO must provide the organizational structure, methods, and tools that will facilitate the delivery of those services. This overall structure must be in place before successful project staffing can occur. Project staffing is related to the success factor "people," discussed in *Chapter 2: The Success Factors*. The overall IT organization must be able to efficiently support both infrastructure initiatives and application implementation initiatives. [Note: We focus on the structure needed for application implementation initiatives. The structure for infrastructure initiatives will not be discussed in this book.]

It seems that organizations are restructuring on a too frequent basis. The tendency when building organization charts is to base them on which *person* should be where, instead of by *function*. People come and go—the functions provided by the organization change less frequently.

A better name for the organization chart is a function chart. A function chart is completed with people's names, but is started by looking solely at the functions that should exist. The function chart should clearly reflect the services that will be offered to the IT organization's customers. This structure mirrors the services provided by the IT organization and it provides an environment in which people can operate. Customers are able to understand the organization and communication flows because the structure is based primarily on the service offerings.

Teams should be established for related functions. This helps the customer use the services more efficiently. In the book titled *The Wisdom of Teams*, Katzenbach and Smith (1993) offer a definition of "team" well suited for client/server development—"a small number of people with complementary skills who are committed to a common purpose....[1]"

The physical implementation of our recommended structure will vary from organization to organization, based primarily on its size. Larger organizations may need entire departments or divisions to staff and manage each function. For example, there may be an application development department and a quality assurance department. These departments or di-

---

[1]Katzenbach, Jon, and Douglas Smith. *The Wisdom of Teams*, pp. 2–3. Boston, MA: Harvard Business School Press, 1993.

visions may not even report to the same person. The specific duties of the CIO will also vary based on the size of your company. When reading this section, do not focus on how the people are placed in your organization. Focus on what functions they perform. Does your organization provide all these functions?

The IT organization poised for success must provide the following application development functions or services:

- Proactive customer relationship management
- Assessment of an organization's current situation, its needs, and possible solutions
- Strategic analysis and planning for application implementations, including the development infrastructure
- Quality assurance for processes, plans, and products
- Delivery of technology solutions to meet business needs
- Development and maintenance of the development infrastructure

These functions are necessary to support the full development lifecycle—from project conception to application roll-out. If any of these functions are not adequately staffed and performed, chaos will reign.

These functions are best performed by teams of people focused on delivering groups of functions. The teams include:

- Business Liaison
- Consulting
- Integration & Development

Projects are completed in stages by people from each of these teams. The project development effort becomes a series of transitions between teams, a passing of the baton from one player to the next. This approach requires cross-team communication and teamwork, which are not bad things!

In order for these teams to be successful, the CIO must do more than build a new organization chart. The CIO must demonstrate commitment to this organization by clearly defining the positions, providing career growth opportunities, allocating budget and time for necessary training, and hiring the right people.

The Business Liaison Team

The business liaison team is focused on the customer. This team is responsible for establishing and maintaining the relationships between the IT organization and its customers. This is an ongoing function, which is performed at a high-level by the CIO. At the lower level, the business liaisons manage the day-to-day relationships. The team is staffed with people who understand the potential of technology when applied to a business problem. They have excellent interpersonal skills, are able to speak to the customer and the developer in language both can understand, and they have a good sense of the business. They clearly understand their customer's business needs and can suggest methods by which IT can provide a solution.

The business liaison team is the customer satisfaction arm of the IT organization. The business liaison is the first line of communication for the customer. It is the responsibility of the business liaison to know what services the customer is receiving and to communicate any problems they are having to the appropriate team. In a sales organization, this role is typically known as the account manager.

The business liaison team also assists the CIO in effective planning and utilization of IT resources. Every several months, a disciplined planning cycle should be completed, initiated by the business liaison team. During this planning process, the business liaison team asks customers what they need and when they need it. They discuss current problems they are having and anticipated changes to business processes or rules. They review the status of applications that were recently deployed and identify critical changes. During these discussions, potential projects are identified and evaluated for the impact on the overall business. The business liaison team, with the customers, creates a list of possible projects, their business rationale, anticipated due dates (based on business requirements), and resource types needed. They then channel that information to the other teams and pro-active planning occurs.

Using a disciplined planning approach, the business liaison team uncovers projects, which may have been "surprise projects," using a less disciplined approach. In many companies, planning and project prioritization is done using the "squeaky wheel" technique—the customer that is the loudest gets their projects done first. This approach is not effective at supporting the overall business direction of the company.

The business liaison team turns project planning into portfolio planning—looking at the overall list of needs and fulfilling the ones most critical to the business. Then, resources are allocated according to what makes sense for the overall business. The business liaison assists in the process by being aware of the customers' needs and anticipating when IT resources may be needed. In some cases, the business liaison team may even lead a steering committee that helps determine overall project priorities. The committee consists of managers from each of the business units. The committee then decides, based on overall business needs, what projects are most important. Even though some individual customers may not get what they want, the overall business gets what it needs.

Example—Financial Investment Company

The CIO and senior-level project manager were holding a meeting with one of their more demanding customers. The objective of the meeting was to more fully understand the current requirements for IT support and future development needs. As the meeting progressed, it was clear that the business unit was not utilizing some applications as much as was anticipated, and that others were being used more. The biggest revelation, however, was that the business unit was about to start their largest annual process and was expecting several systems to be available—within the next six weeks! Surprise! The IT people had not heard of the systems, had no plans to build them, and more importantly, had no resources to complete them by the expected timeframe. The CIO asked the business manager who in the IT organization had received this request for systems, and when. The business manager replied, "You did. Just now. No one has asked us like this before. We just tell them and they make it happen somehow. Isn't that normal?"

An organization without a business liaison function has no chance to satisfy customers, regardless of project successes. The IT organization is functioning in a constant state of chaos and customers are not receiving the best service. As a result, the entire business suffers.

The Consulting Team

The consulting team is the next team the customer sees during the development lifecycle. The business liaison develops a high-level definition of the problem and creates a conceptual description of the solution. The consulting team then transitions from the business liaison team and takes the solution to the next level of detail. The consulting team is staffed with experienced IT professionals, people with excellent architecture skills. They are able to understand the "big picture" and see how the problem fits into that view. They do not delve into the details of the problem or solution immediately but, instead, focus on the implications the solution has on the organization's portfolio of applications. They are able to look at a problem, see similarities to other problems, and recommend a solution.

The consulting team is involved in the conceptual design, application scoping, and project definition phases of the development lifecycle. They are also involved in the requirements-gathering and initial analysis phases of a project. The consulting team provides a technical architect and functional architect, who are skilled in technology strategy, business process re-engineering, and cost/benefit analysis techniques. This team assesses the customer's current situation and needs and recommends a solution. The solution may be the implementation of a package, the development of a new application, or changes in business processes. In many cases, the consulting team will play a lead role in the package selection process.

The members of the consulting team move quickly from project to project. They are not involved in long-term (6 month or more) projects. They are the "swat team"—they come in, quickly assess the situation, draw upon their vast experiences, outline the solution, then hand off to the next team. They provide consistency and cohesion between the various application implementation initiatives. They are architecting a common framework for the other teams to use.

The Integration & Development Team

The integration and development team then takes the baton from the consulting team. This team provides the majority of the people for staffing the project. Other people will come from the end-user departments, the business liaison team, the consulting team, and teams based on the infrastructure initiative side of the IT organization. This team is staffed with strong analysts, designers, developers, testers, and technical writers.

The integration and development team is responsible for the delivery of solutions to the customer's business needs. This includes the selection, customization, and integration of packaged solutions, as well as the development of custom applications. The resources within this team flow from integration responsibilities to development tasks, depending on project demands. This team also provides maintenance functions for existing applications, based on requests received by a Help Desk area. Additionally, this team is responsible for building, maintaining, and supporting the development infrastructure. They complete the work started by the consulting team and carry it through implementation. The business liaison team then continues the application's lifecycle by picking up after implementation.

The integration and development team is the primary focus of this book because it is responsible for the delivery of solutions to the customer's business needs. This includes the selection and integration of packaged solutions, as well as the development of custom applications. The resources on this team will flow from integration responsibilities to development tasks, depending on project demands. This team also provides maintenance functions for existing applications, based on requests received by the Help Desk.

Table 3–1 describes responsibilities for the integration and development team.

TABLE 3–1. INTEGRATION AND DEVELOPMENT
TEAM RESPONSIBILITIES

Responsibilities

Application Development:

- Requirements-gathering and analysis
- Package selection
- Package customization (design, coding, testing)
- Custom software development (design, coding, testing)
- Integration of new applications with existing applications
- End-user and support team training
- Documentation development and delivery

Maintenance:

- Track change requests; identify release schedule and scope for each release
- Complete bug fixes and enhancements
- Develop intermediate to complex ad-hoc (limited use) reports/queries
- Respond to tier-3 application support requests: answer intermediate to complex questions on functions in the application
- Provide conversion assistance to customers

Project-specific staffing guidance is provided in *Chapter 4: Building the Best Team.*

CREATING THE TECHNOLOGY STRATEGY

The "technology" success factor is defined in *Chapter 2: The Success Factors* as "the development and use of a technology strategy to help select the components of the deployment environment." The deployment environment is the technical environment in which the applications will run. During the development lifecycle, the project team assesses the business needs and chooses the most appropriate combination of technologies in which to present the solution. If a technology strategy does not exist, the result will be an assortment of platforms and products, each requiring a unique set of skills to support. This creates chaos in the long-term life of the IT organization (as well as in the end-user community). To avoid this problem, the CIO must develop a strategy for the direction of technology use. The strategy includes the basic parameters and fundamental decisions about the technologies to be used and their implementation.

A strategy is defined as "A plan of action ... intended to accomplish a specific goal" (The American Heritage Dictionary). The primary goal is to provide technology solutions to business needs; this is defined by the statement of purpose. Secondary goals include:

- Providing a list of acceptable components for use
- Simplifying the deployment environments for the end-user community and the IT organization
- Utilizing best-of-breed technology components
- Remaining technically current

The CIO must ensure that the technology strategy exists, is current, and is used. The strategy must be reviewed and updated on a periodic basis, at least annually. Along with an understanding of the business needs, it should be the basis for all technology decisions.

The technology strategy must contain the following information:

- ■ A summary of what technologies are in use today:

  This inventory provides the background for the current state. It is the basis for any migration plans and also helps to explain why certain technologies are part of the strategy.

- ■ A summary of the current state of the industry:

  This summary briefly describes the market share leaders and industry trends. It helps to explain why certain technologies are part of the strategy.

- ■ A statement of general direction, relative to the industry direction:

  This statement is the core of the technology strategy and describes the overall approach to selecting technology components. It is the general philosophy and conceptual approach that indicates how technology is viewed by the organization—is it an opportunity or a cost? This statement describes whether cutting-edge products should be used as opposed to more proven products with certain market share.

- ■ A list of options for each development environment component:

  This part of the strategy is used most often by the project teams, especially the technical architects. This list defines the various options allowed for each component (see Figure 3–1) and the rationale for selecting each option. This list requires frequent updates triggered by changes in vendors' directions, industry trends, product market shares, and experience.

  This list is also accompanied by guides for selecting one option over another. For example, there would be rationale for choosing a specific client platform. The sales force

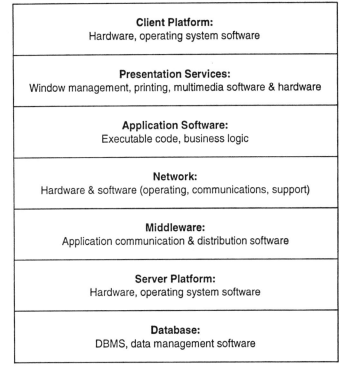

FIGURE 3–1. Deployment environment components.

may need different hardware and operating systems software than the accounting department.

Finally, this list is accompanied by descriptions of allowable exceptions. This section defines situations where the selected options do not need to be used. For example, a packaged solution may be available only on certain platforms that are not part of the technology strategy. An exception may be allowed if the package meets more requirements than any other package, and if the package requires minimal technical support and operations skills.

■ A migration plan (for supporting existing technologies and migrating to new):

A migration plan should be included in the technology strategy. The migration plan describes, at a high-level, how legacy technologies (mainframe, PC, first-generation client/server) will be migrated to, or integrated with, those indicated in the technology strategy. The plan will include support and operational approaches, deadlines for migration, and rationale for not migrating to newer technologies.

The technology strategy contains a large amount of information. The CIO must be committed to development and maintenance of this document. Remember, however, that this strategy must always tie to the business. It cannot be focused on using the latest and greatest technology just "because it's there."

It is also not enough for a strategy to exist. The CIO must be committed to following it and ensure that the project teams are following the strategy. The CIO cannot allow exceptions for every project—that results in chaos over the long-term! Also, the CIO must support this strategy through the establishment of the development environment. Changing the technical direction of the organization will impact the IT organization; the CIO must be committed to spending the money upgrading the development tools and the skills of the IT team.

SUMMARY

The CIO has a critical job to do and, today, not much time in which to do it. Client/server development presents new challenges to the IT organization. For the IT team to succeed, the CIO must develop and implement success strategies. Use of the proper people, process, technology, and tools will only be possible if the CIO:

- Ties technology solutions to business needs
- Properly structures the Information Technology organization
- Creates the technology strategy

PART 2

PREPARING FOR PROJECT SUCCESS

CHAPTER 4

BUILDING THE BEST TEAM

Skill:
Proficiency, ability, or dexterity; expertness

Role:
A function or position

Today's business and technical environments have changed the life of the software development team. Downsizing, budget constraints, tighter deadlines, and more sophisticated business requirements demand more complex systems faster. Client/server technology, while enabling the implementation of better business solutions, have created an environment of challenge. New tasks are required to build these systems and these tasks require a new set of skills and roles.

Today's software development team is expected to provide business expertise, technical wizardry, and management magic. Software developers are being forced to work effectively on teams of adaptable, functionally, and technically diverse people, all wearing different "hats" on any given day.

Today's software development teams, instead of knowing a small number of stable technologies, must understand a number of different technologies and tools that are constantly changing. You can read about these personnel requirements in the trade magazines weekly. You can also read about the extreme difference between supply and demand for those possessing the "hot skills" of the day.

This "people" factor of client/server implementation is critical for the success of projects. For the Information Technology (IT) organization, people are its most important asset. Building effective software is still a labor-intensive process that requires unique skills and the ability to work productively in teams. While people can be hired with the right technical skills, they will not have the understanding of the specific business terminology, culture, and unstated requirements.

Many IT organizations, and the people working within these organizations, are questioning the value of the skills obtained in past years. "What do we do with people who have mainframe skills? How can they be used on client/server projects? What value do we place on these skills?"

Industry studies have shown that some mainframe programmers will not migrate successfully to the world of client/server; however, the majority will make the transition. The core skills required to build mainframe or PC-based applications are still the core skills needed to build client/server applications. These skills include the ability to:

- Complete deliverables according to a specified development process
- Gather and analyze requirements
- Translate requirements into models then into designs
- Identify unique blocks of functions and code
- Develop efficient code in various programming languages, or use various programming tools
- Analyze and test an application against specifications
- Manage scope, schedule, budget, and resources

Client/server development does not negate these core skills—it slightly modifies them. For example, the programming languages and development tools used in client/server applications will be different from mainframe applications. The development process will have some additional tasks and deliverables. There are many new skills required because of the technical capabilities involved in client/server development. Today, a client/server project may need people with the ability to build reusable architecture objects in programming languages such as C++. Tasks and skills such as this translate to new roles for client/server projects.

This chapter reviews the unique skills and roles needed for the development of client/server applications. It is important to differentiate between skills, tasks, roles, and people. Focusing on skills and roles will help to analyze staffing requirements abstractly, without being tied to titles or individuals.

THE STAFFING PUZZLE

Skills are the building blocks of the staffing puzzle. Skills describe the proficiencies or abilities that are required to complete

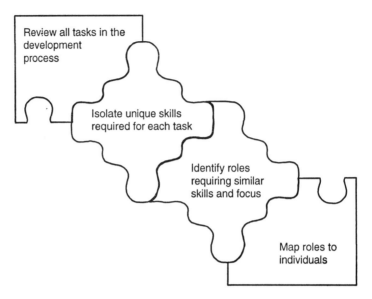

FIGURE 4–1. Pieces of the staffing puzzle.

specific tasks. The staffing process is illustrated in Figure 4–1. The required skills are identified by analyzing all the tasks involved in client/server development. The skills are then organized by role. A role simply represents a collection of skills that have responsibility for completing specific tasks; a role does not represent a specific individual. Roles are determined by identifying tasks that require the same skills and have a common focus.

For example, there are several tasks involved in the analysis, design, and testing of the graphical user interface (GUI), something that is generally developed for a client/server application. These tasks require the following skills (not a comprehensive list):

■ An understanding of usability principles
■ A knowledge of GUI design standards
■ A proficiency in interviewing techniques

■ An ability to read and understand analysis deliverables, such as data flow diagrams, object models, data models, event models, etc.

■ A proficiency with the window painting tools used on the project

■ An ability to develop and execute usability test plans

By analyzing all the tasks and the associated skills, several roles are identified, including a role of "Interface Designer." The Interface Designer has the following responsibilities (not a comprehensive list):

■ To create design documents for the windows of the application, based on analysis deliverables

■ To obtain feedback on window designs, through prototyping, usability test, review sessions, and interviews

■ To develop the test plans for the complete user interface, including the windows, help, and documentation

Once all the roles are identified, they are mapped to individuals. The timing of each role and the skills of each individual are the major inputs to this step. This level of analysis is helpful in determining what training is needed, what types of individuals should be hired, and what types of external resources should be purchased. Table 4–1 lists some guidelines for assigning individuals to roles.

This analysis of tasks, skills, roles, and people must be completed, to some extent, for every project. The tasks and required skills vary from project to project; they are dependent on the methodology, tools, and techniques used and the technology and functionality being implemented.

The sections below describe the various categories of roles involved in client/server projects. The responsibilities of each category are defined, the roles belonging to the category are

TABLE 4–1. STAFFING GUIDELINES

- All responsibilities must be accounted for by someone on the project team.
- Formality of roles will vary, based on project duration, project complexity, and project size; a longer project requires more formal assigning of roles than a shorter project.
- Roles should be assigned to people based on skills, not titles.
- Corporate culture must be acknowledged when assigning people to roles; some organizations do not allow people to work outside their defined position or job title.
- A role can be filled by one or many people.
- A person can fill one or many roles; if a person fills more than one role, the roles should focus on similar areas of the project or utilize similar skills.
- Consider an individual's existing skills, interests, training needs, and long-term goals when assigning a person to a role.
- When assigning external people (consultants and contractors) to roles, assess the current availability of in-house skills, the long-term cost and benefit of developing those skills in-house, and the risk involved in placing external people in critical roles.

listed, and the skills required for client/server development are described.

MANAGEMENT ROLES

The management roles are responsible for providing direction and taking responsibility for some portion of the project. Each of the roles provides direction for a different level or tier of the project. All these roles have valuable input to the overall project schedule, scope, and availability of resources.

The management roles are listed and described in Table 4–2.

Communication between these management roles is essential to the project because the actions of each of these roles affects the others. For example, a delay in hardware from a ven-

TABLE 4–2. MANAGEMENT ROLES

Role	Primary Responsibilities
Executive Sponsor	■ Provide high-level overall direction for the project: scope, schedule, budget, and staffing. ■ Resolve major issues related to project parameters: scope, schedule, etc.
Project Manager	■ Provide day-to-day direction for the project: develop schedules and budgets; assign teams and workload; resolve and escalate issues; report on status and issues.
End-User Manager	■ Obtain, direct, and maintain end-user involvement in the project: schedules, team and workload assignments, and status reporting. ■ Resolve scope issues with the project manager, primarily by providing functional input and cost/benefit analysis.
Team Leader	■ Provide day-to-day direction for the team: maintain schedules and budgets; assign workload; resolve and escalate issues; report on status and issues.
Vendor Liaison	■ Coordinate all vendor (hardware, software, training, consulting) activities: delivery schedules, staffing, quality reviews, and invoice approval.
Infrastructure Liaison	■ Ensure services are received from infrastructure group. ■ Convey information from infrastructure group to project team on changes in standards, etc.
Project Advisor	■ Provide feedback and advice on concerns of project manager. ■ Notify project manager of events (good and bad) on other projects that may help manage current project.
Management Support	■ Provide all support functions: project management tool administration and data entry, status report generation and data-gathering, etc.

dor, an area managed by the vendor liaison, may impact the overall project schedule, an area managed by the project manager. Therefore, communication is necessary between these two roles to develop the appropriate action plan.

The roles of project manager, vendor liaison, and infrastructure liaison may be filled comfortably by one person (depending on project size and complexity), and at best by someone from the IT organization. It is preferred, however, that the person filling the end-user manager role comes from the end-user community served by the application.

Managing client/server applications requires several new skills for the management roles. Most importantly, the management roles must understand the technical environment in which the application will be deployed. The high-level technical requirements must be determined before completing scope definition and estimating costs, benefits, timelines, and resource requirements. Management must also understand the complexities and implications of problems with the architecture components to effectively escalate issues and refine timelines.

The vendor liaison role is especially important in client/server development because there can be large numbers of vendors whose activities must be coordinated. The infrastructure liaison role is also critical to client/server development. Changes to the client/server deployment environment can severely impact the applications architecture. Tight communication is required between these two teams to minimize re-work and errors.

Client/server development requires the project manager to be able to manage a more iterative development process. Client/server applications cannot effectively be developed using a traditional phased approach, but instead are best developed using a process of iteration and overlap. The various tasks and deliverables are tightly integrated and a change in one area can affect many other areas. Management must understand this development approach and the implications of these changes.

FUNCTIONAL ROLES

The functional roles are responsible for delivering the business functions of the application. They provide all the input and analysis of the business functions of the application. Their focus is on *what* functions the application will provide.

The functional roles are listed and described in Table 4–3.

TABLE 4–3. FUNCTIONAL ROLES

Role	Primary Responsibilities
Business Specialist	■ Provide input, review, and feedback on: business terminology, business function requirements, end-user profiles, usability requirements, technical implementation, and requirements.
Functional Architect	■ Define the scope of the functional components of the application. ■ Ensure that the application will solve the business problems presented. ■ Describe the technical architecture to the other functional roles; ensure that designs are feasible, given the technologies selected.
Functional Analyst	■ Gather functional requirements from business specialists, industry experts, etc. ■ Analyze requirements from object, data, process, and events views; develop associated models. ■ Work with technical architect, technical analyst, database architect to verify requirements are feasible.
Functional Designer	■ Translate models into designs for use by the functional interface and technical teams. ■ Design test cases and data.
Functional Programmer	■ Develop code that provides the business functionality and reusable components.
Functional Tester	■ Test the business components of the application and ensure they provide the required business functionality, as defined by the business specialist.

During the scoping and requirement gathering tasks of the development process, the business specialist, functional architect, and functional analyst:

■ Define the business terminology used
■ Complete the end-user profiles
■ Define business rules, conditions, and calculations
■ Identify the business objects and data needed
■ Identify business processes and events
■ Work with the technical roles to determine the overall application framework

The functional architect, functional analyst, and functional designer are then responsible for the functional analysis and design, or translation, of the requirements into models and then design specifications. These deliverables are used during design, prototyping, and testing by other members of the development team.

During construction, functional programmers develop the business components of the application, using their knowledge of the business rules, data, events, and end-user profiles. They focus on implementing the business functionality and creating reusable business components. As business components are completed and combined, the functional tester performs functional testing—verifying that the application is providing the business functions as they are needed.

The functional roles are the least affected by the client/server development process. Their responsibilities are focused on the implementation of the business functionality in the application, not its technical implementation. The people filling the functional roles need to be familiar with the basic client/server technologies being implemented so they know what is feasible. The roles of business specialist, functional designer, functional analyst, and functional tester can be filled by people from the end-user organization. They will need to be familiar with the software development process and the appropriate associated techniques. They also need to be able to use the documentation, development, and testing tools selected for the project. Staffing these roles with end-users is an excellent way to leverage their business expertise and improve the chances for the project's success. Refer to *Chapter 9: Defining the Details* for more details.

INTERFACE ROLES

The graphical user interface (GUI) has proven to be an important component of the client/server application. There are productivity and training benefits of using a GUI instead of a character-based user interface. The user interface of an application involves more than the windows; it also involves the on-line help, hard-copy documentation (manuals and binders), and training materials. To the application's end-user, the user interface *is* the application.

The interface roles are listed and described in Table 4–4.

The interface roles focus on designing, developing, and testing all aspects of the user interface. These roles work closely with the functional roles. In fact, the same people can fill both functional and interface roles, if they possess the necessary skills.

The business specialist, functional architect, and functional analyst define the business functions that must be supported (objects/data, processes, and events). The interface architect, with assistance from the functional architect, designs the interface framework. The interface designer then designs the windows to best implement the business functions. The interface architect also determines what windows and application functions are best supported by various styles of on-line help or hard-copy documentation. The interface architect also provides a conceptual design for the documentation and training, determining how information will be presented, through which medium, and providing the outline for the instructional designer. The instructional designer and technical writer are re-

TABLE 4–4. INTERFACE ROLES

Role	Primary Responsibilities
Interface Architect	■ Gather interface, on-line help, documentation and training requirements from business specialists, including industry experts, etc. ■ Analyze interface requirements and design the application's overall look-and-feel; identify primary menu items and windows. ■ Create conceptual design of on-line help, documentation, and training. ■ Describe the interface architecture to the other interface roles; ensure that designs are feasible, given the technologies selected.
Interface Designer	■ Identify and design all windows of the application. ■ Identify the structure of user help (on-line and hard-copy); identify critical areas for training. ■ Design test cases and data.
Interface Programmer	■ Develop code that provides the full graphical user interface and reusable components.
Usability Tester	■ Test all the interface components of the application and ensure they provide maximum usability and adherence to User Interface (UI) standards.
Instructional Designer	■ Design and develop training materials.
Technical Writer	■ Design and develop hard-copy documentation and on-line help.
Trainer	■ Deliver training.

sponsible for the detailed design and development of the on-line help, hard-copy documentation, and training materials.

Specialized skills are required for the development of the overall interface and have changed significantly with client/server systems. In some senses, these roles have been affected the most with the migration to client/server development. These roles also have the greatest impact on the application's quality, as perceived by the end-users.

The interface architect, interface designer, interface programmer, and usability tester must be experts in GUI design and the principles of usability. They must be focused on providing the required business functions in a usable and *technically feasible* manner. Some organizations feel that the interface designer should ignore the technical constraints completely, thus providing the most user-friendly interface possible. The approach used by the interface designer should be determined primarily by the corporate culture and the project constraints.

The other interface roles must still have solid skills in instructional design and technical writing; however, they must also know how to best design and develop on-line help. GUI applications provide many opportunities for on-line help, including help files, message bar help, wizards, and context-sensitive help. Training can be provided through wizards and context-sensitive help, as well as through multi-media functions. People with the skills for these roles can be staffed from external sources, with minimal risk to the project completion. The interface designer and usability tester roles, however, should be staffed internally as much as possible.

TECHNICAL ROLES

The technical roles are responsible for all technical aspects of the application. These roles are responsible for determining, designing, developing, testing, and tuning the application's architecture and associated components. Technical roles bridge the gap between the interface and business components and the architecture.

The technical roles are listed and described in Table 4–5.

The technical architect and technical analyst are responsible for gathering the technical requirements and determining the technology most appropriate for implementing the application. These roles develop guidelines for dividing the application into layers and provide the overall application framework.

TABLE 4–5. TECHNICAL ROLES

Role	Primary Responsibilities
Technical Architect	■ Design the application's architecture framework: layers, trade-offs, and reusability parameters. ■ Determine the appropriate technology to meet the technical and functional requirements. ■ Describe the architecture to the other team members; ensure that designs are feasible, given the technologies selected.
Technical Analyst	■ Gather technical requirements from business specialists, industry experts, etc. ■ Analyze technical requirements; develop associated architecture models; verify requirements are feasible.
Technical Designer	■ Translate models into designs of the system architecture. ■ Design test cases and data.
Database Architect	■ Design and develop the physical databases implemented. ■ Work with functional analyst, functional designer, and interface designer to provide feasible, optimized database accesses.
Technical Programmer	■ Develop code that provides the architecture functionality and reusable components.
Technical Tester	■ Test the architecture components of the application and ensure they provide the required technical functionality, as defined by the technical architect.
Reusability Liaison	■ Working with the technical architect, determine project's approach towards reusability. ■ Identify components (technical, interface, and functional) from other applications for use in this application. ■ Identify reusable components for use in other applications.
Technical Support	■ Provide support and coordination for development environment; will vary based on the organization—may include administrator functions, support functions, or coordination.

The technical roles are more specialized and critical for client/server development than for traditional mainframe development. These roles are just as important as the functional roles for the overall development of the application, and require deep technical skills, as well as a basic understanding of the business functions to be implemented. The technical architect must have a "big-picture" view and communicate that view to the other roles. These roles require a knowledge of all the components of the client/server architecture: networking, communications, middleware, hardware, operating software, etc. They also must understand the organization's goals towards reusability and be able to identify and develop reusable components.

As an organization moves to client/server development, many of the technical roles will be staffed with external experts. This is an effective method of completing the project with qualified people, however, the resources to maintain and support the application need to be developed during the project. Knowledge transfer and skills building should be considered a vital part of the project. The project manager and team leaders must schedule project time to complete these additional tasks. Project schedules should also include time to adequately document the application's components, including code. Most importantly, every team member must ensure that they learned what they need to know prior to any external experts leaving the project.

SUMMARY

When determining the staffing of a client/server project, you should first look at the skills required to complete the specific tasks within the project. Once skills are assessed, organize them by role. Determine the roles by identifying tasks that require the same skill sets. When all the roles are identified, assign individuals to each role. The timing of each role and the skills of each individual are major inputs to your decisions.

General categories of roles involved in client/server projects include:

- Management roles
- Functional roles
- Interface roles
- Technical roles

Proper staffing, assigning the right people to the right roles, based on their skills, will greatly increase a project's chances for success.

CHAPTER 5

FOLLOWING THE RIGHT PROCESS

Process:
A series of operations performed in the making
or treatment of a product

The process of developing client/server applications is new to most chief information officers (CIOs), project managers, and software developers. There are new issues to address, new deliverables to create, and new tasks to complete that were not necessary when developing for the mainframe or PC. For example, building the architecture for a mainframe or PC application does not require as many steps as implementing a three-tiered client/server architecture. When a team does not have significant experience developing client/server applications, they are not aware of these new issues, tasks, and deliverables, so a formal development process becomes critical to success.

The CIO and project manager are responsible for ensuring that the appropriate development process, or methodology, is available for the project to use. That is part of "preparing for project success." In order for them to have the right process available, they must understand:

- Methodology definition and benefits
- General development process
- Development approaches
- Client/server methodology requirements
- Methodology selection process

DEFINING "METHODOLOGY"

Chapter 2: The Success Factors discussed the need for following a recipe when first making a pie. You are not sure of all the steps, ingredients, or timings. A recipe provides you with guidance until you are proficient in the process. When first building a client/server application, you need to closely follow a recipe, or methodology. A methodology is simply a formalization of a process, whether it is making a pie, constructing a mall, developing training materials, or implementing a client/server business solution. For purposes of this chapter, a methodology is the collection of specific steps, deliverables, and techniques that are used to deliver an application.

In addition to providing guidance to the project team, a methodology provides these other benefits:

■ Packaged expertise
■ Training
■ Consistency
■ Improved communication

A methodology gives the organization migrating to client/server a "leg up" on the learning curve. When you purchase a commercial methodology, you are buying the knowledge and expertise of the vendor. Most methodology vendors have invested significant amounts of money into research on industry best practices. They packaged the results of that research into a certain format and make it available (for a price, of course!) to your organization. Instead of learning how to build client/server projects by trial and error, you can take advantage of this packaged expertise.

Using a methodology also provides a level of training. Reading and practicing the techniques described in the methodology provides on-the-job training. Many times, we have seen project team members "surf" their project's methodology and learn new terminology and techniques. This informal training has minimal cost in terms of time away from the project. Also, the knowledge gained is applied immediately.

In addition to providing packaged expertise and on-the-job training, a methodology provides consistency within and across projects. A methodology is a type of standard, and standards strive to provide consistency. A methodology provides consistency in how the project teams use terminology, define task names, populate deliverables, utilize techniques, and estimate projects. Because the entire project team is using the same terminology and completing the same tasks using the same techniques, it is much easier to incorporate new team members. It is also easier to move people from one project to another and have them quickly become familiar with the project.

From a management perspective, using a methodology allows for projects to be managed consistently. Estimating and budgeting can be done the same way from project to project, making it much easier to compare "apples to apples."

Finally, using a methodology can improve communication, within projects and across projects. A methodology provides a forum for communicating the "lessons learned" on one project to another. For example, if one project identifies a technique that works well for prioritizing requirements, it can be added to the methodology and used on following projects.

A methodology can also improve communication since everyone is using the same terminology between themselves and the end-users. We have seen many projects stumble because team members were not using consistent terminology for task names and deliverables. Imagine how an overall development organization looks to the end-user community if every project uses different terminology and deliverable templates for the same basic task!

Example—Real Estate Investment Company

This company's application development was completed by three competing development organizations, each building systems for the same customers. Each development organization built systems following their own various methodologies. The business community was very concerned by the lack of consistency in approach from each of the development organizations. Across projects, their roles changed, terminology was not consistent, and major deliverables differed drastically. Project estimating and management was also handled differently from organization to organization. Because of the time required to understand each development organization's process, the business community assigned certain people to work only with certain development organizations—this created major resource constraints and risks for projects.

Another major problem caused by the lack of consistency between the development organizations was the attitudes of the people towards each other. Each development organization felt the other was incompetent—the others weren't doing things "the right way." The business community thought all three groups were incompetent and wanted to outsource their development projects to external vendors.

At this point, a decision was made to integrate the three different organizations into one application development organization, where consistency in the process was a major goal.

THE GENERAL DEVELOPMENT PROCESS

There is more than one valid way to build a client/server application. Different tasks and deliverables are needed based on the project's parameters. For example, creating a custom solution requires different steps than purchasing and implementing a packaged solution. However, all projects will follow a similar, general development process.

In the engineering world, the development process is described as "analyze, design, build, evaluate." Figure 5–1 illustrates this process. Analyze refers to the process of determining the problem to be solved and the exploration of various solutions. Design is the process of defining the solution in concrete

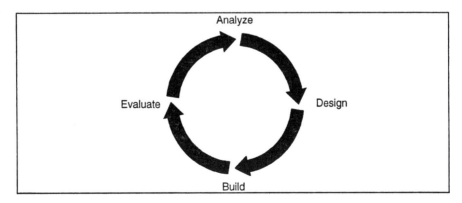

FIGURE 5–1.   The general development process.

terms. Build is the process of building the solution and testing it. Evaluate refers to the process of reviewing the solution and determining when it is no longer appropriate in its given state.

This general engineering principle is the foundation for the software development process. Each of the four stages in this general process corresponds to one or more stages in the software development process. Table 5–1 shows the relationship between the stages in each process.

Table 5–2 describes each stage in the development process and lists the key deliverables of each. The stages are discussed in much more detail throughout *Part III: Client/Server Success Techniques.*

Figure 5–2 illustrates this software development process. Each bar represents one of the primary stages in the process. There is overlap between the stages; which is explained in more detail in *Chapter 7: Managing Chaos.*

DEVELOPMENT APPROACHES

As we mentioned above, there are several acceptable variations on the general software development process. These variations are referred to as development approaches. A development ap-

TABLE 5–1. COMPARISON OF STAGES IN THE DEVELOPMENT PROCESSES

General Development Process	Software Development Process
Analyze	■ Requirements-Gathering ■ Analysis
Design	■ Design
Build	■ Construction ■ Testing ■ Implementation
Evaluate	■ Requirements-Gathering (after a period of use and maintenance)

TABLE 5–2. STAGES IN THE SOFTWARE DEVELOPMENT PROCESSES

Objectives	Key Deliverables
Requirements-Gathering: ■ Identify functional, interface, and technical requirements of the application ■ Determine the scope of the current release ■ Identify objectives for following releases	■ Scope document, including requirements descriptions ■ Project budget, timeline, and staffing plan ■ Cost/benefit analysis ■ Release schedule
Analysis: ■ Develop a true knowledge of the end-user's requirements ■ Understand all implications of the functional, interface, and technical requirements	■ Object model ■ Data model ■ Event model ■ Process model ■ Dialog Navigation model ■ Architecture model
Design: ■ Describe all aspects of the application in concrete terms	■ User interface design, including documentation and training outlines ■ Database design ■ Architecture design ■ Application logic design
Construction: ■ Build the physical components of the application	■ Code ■ End-user documentation ■ System documentation ■ Training materials
Testing: ■ Ensure all components of the application function as required	■ Test plan ■ Test cases ■ Test scenarios ■ Test scripts ■ Change requests
Implementation: ■ Deliver the application to the end-users	■ Implementation schedule ■ Training schedule ■ Installed components

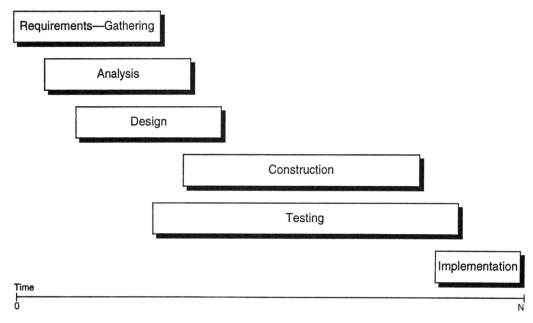

FIGURE 5–2. The software development process.

proach is the general process or style followed in developing an application, dictated by the project's parameters.

One standard approach is not acceptable for all types of projects. Depending on the project's goals, there are different tasks that must be completed and different techniques that should be used.

The three common development approaches are:

■ Maintenance
■ Package selection and implementation
■ Custom development

Table 5–3 defines each development approach and when they should be used.

These three development approaches are different primarily in the tasks completed during the initial stages of the devel-

TABLE 5–3.   DEVELOPMENT APPROACH CHOICES

Approach	Description	When Appropriate
Maintenance	Changes to the existing application are identified, analyzed, designed, integrated, and tested. A new version of the application is then implemented.	An existing application requires functional enhancements, performance improvements, technical modifications, or bug-fixes.
Package Selection and Implementation	Requirements of the new application are gathered and analyzed. Various packages are reviewed and the most appropriate is selected. Then, modifications to the package are designed, coded, and tested. The package and modifications are integrated, tested, and implemented.	A package is available that sufficiently meets the business and technical requirements of the business and is cost-effective.
Custom Development	Requirements of the new application are gathered and analyzed. A solution is then designed, constructed, tested, and implemented.	A package is not available that sufficiently meets the business and technical requirements of the organization; a custom application is built from "scratch."

opment lifecycle. For example, each approach has a "requirements-gathering" stage, but the tasks completed are different. Also, the extent of analysis and design differs between the three approaches.

Before starting the project, it is critical to understand the overall project goals. Then, the appropriate development approach can be selected by asking a series of questions. The first question relates to the existence of an application: *Is the application being developed for initial release, or are modifications being made to an application already in production?*

Maintenance

If modifications are being made to an application already in production, then the project team is delivering a maintenance release. Therefore, a maintenance development approach should be followed. The maintenance approach focuses on gathering, analyzing, and implementing changes to an existing application.

Over time, changes to the application are submitted and logged on change requests. Periodically, the change requests are reviewed. The criticalness of the change, the impact on the overall application, any benefits from additional functionality, and the costs of making the change are all considered. They are "bundled" and scheduled for a release. The changes are then treated as requirements. They are further analyzed in order to determine how to smoothly integrate the new or modified functionality into the existing database, code, documentation, and training.

Then, the new or modified application components are designed, coded, and tested. Documentation and training materials are modified or created if necessary. When all the development tasks are complete, the improved application (whole or just parts) is released. It may be installed by the end-users or an installation/maintenance team.

Package Selection and Implementation

If the project is not going to modify an existing application, it is developing an application for initial release. At this point, the next question is: *Based on what we currently know, can the required functionality be met by an application that is available on the commercial market?*

If the answer to this question is yes, the package selection and implementation approach should be followed. Packages exist for many of a company's non-competitive functions, such as human resources, payroll, general ledger, etc.

In this approach:

■ Functional, interface, and technical requirements are gathered and analyzed.

■ Candidate packages are reviewed against these requirements.

■ The most appropriate package is selected and tested.

■ Changes needed to the package are identified and designed.

■ Interfaces to other applications are identified and designed.

■ Modifications are coded and tested.

■ Training materials and documentation are developed.

■ End-users are trained.

■ The complete, integrated package is tested and accepted by the end-users.

■ The package is installed, configured, and rolled-out.

Custom Development

If a suitable packaged solution is not available, the application must then be "built from scratch." The project team may know before the project starts that a package does not exist. In other cases, the project team may discover part-way through the package selection process that an appropriate package does not exist and a custom solution is required. Traditionally, most applications were created using a custom development approach.

In this approach:

■ Functional, interface, and technical requirements are gathered and analyzed.

■ Functional, interface, and technical components of the application are designed.

■ Functional, interface, and technical components are constructed and tested.

■ Training materials and documentation are developed.

■ End-users are trained.

■ The complete application is tested and accepted by the end-users.

■ The application is installed, configured, and rolled-out.

The custom development approach is very similar to the package selection and implementation approach. What differs between the two approaches is the level of detail and the volume. In the custom approach, analysis, design, coding, and testing are conducted in much more depth and breadth than in the package approach. When implementing a package, this level of work has already been completed by the package vendor. When the project team is building the application from "the ground up," they must complete the work themselves.

Development Approaches and Methodology

Each development approach requires a unique methodology. While there are common elements between development approaches, a methodology is only truly appropriate for one development approach. Using a custom application development methodology for a package selection project is like using a hammer to get a square peg to fit into a round hole. Not a technique recommended for the hole, the peg, or the person hammering! Some methodology products claim to support all types of development, but they do so at the expense of providing details. Those details are what provides the guidance to the project team.

Therefore, a development organization needs three client/server development methodologies—one for each development approach. If your organization is still developing or maintaining host-based applications, you will also need corresponding host-based methodologies.

CLIENT/SERVER METHODOLOGY REQUIREMENTS

The stages of the development process are essentially the same for host-based development as they are for client/server development. However, the tasks, roles, responsibilities, deliverable content, and issues are significantly different. Therefore, the methodologies for host-based development efforts are not sufficient for client/server development. They don't address the new skills, tasks, and issues required for client/server applications, such as:

- Using a client/server infrastructure
- Managing iteration and overlap
- Defining application scope and releases
- Maintaining a user-centered viewpoint
- Analyzing business objects
- Prototyping effectively
- Understanding GUI design implications
- Incorporating technical requirements
- Building a client/server architecture
- Identifying technical objects and re-use opportunities
- Testing client/server applications
- Testing for usability
- Configuring and rolling-out successfully

These issues are discussed in detail throughout *Part III: Client/Server Success Techniques.*

SELECTING A METHODOLOGY

The project manager is responsible for selecting the methodology that is used on the project. The primary step in defining a process for client/server development is to determine the appropriate development approach. Should the development work follow a maintenance approach, package selection and implementation approach, or custom approach? This requires some knowledge of the project's goals and the application's objectives. If this is a new application, there must be enough preliminary work done to determine if a suitable package may be available and desired.

Figure 5–3 summarizes the process for determining the development approach.

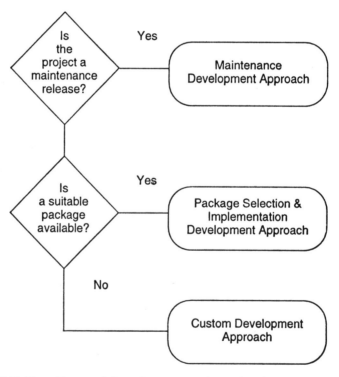

FIGURE 5–3.   Determining the appropriate development approach.

Once the development approach is selected, the project manager then analyzes the corresponding methodology and ensures that it provides adequate support for client/server development. In an ideal world, the development infrastructure exists, including suitable methodologies. The establishment of the development infrastructure, including how to select and purchase its components, are discussed in *Chapter 6: Establishing the Development Infrastructure.*

Once the project manager has selected the methodology, they have enabled the team to "follow the right process."

SUMMARY

Client/server development is new to many project teams. They do not have the experience and expertise required for many of the client/server specific tasks and issues. Therefore, project success is dependent on the use of an appropriate client/server development methodology.

An appropriate client/server development methodology:

■ Is the collection of specific steps, deliverables, and techniques that are used to build the application;

■ Follows the general software development process;

■ Supports the development approach being followed; and

■ Provides guidance on client/server specific tasks, roles, deliverables, and issues.

As long as the methodology you select does these things, you're starting down the right road. A good client/server infrastructure and solid client/server project management skills will keep you from straying.

CHAPTER 6

ESTABLISHING THE DEVELOPMENT INFRASTRUCTURE

Infrastructure:
The basic facilities, services, and installations needed for the functioning of a community or society

Prior to starting any project, it is critical to provide the development team with the necessary tools and environment with which to perform their tasks. This is known as the development infrastructure, or development environment. As defined in *Chapter 2: The Success Factors*, the development environment is a suite of tools, standards, services, and templates used to build and deploy client/server applications. The components of the development environment are used by all project teams. The components are selected based on the technology strategy developed by the Chief Information Officer (CIO). Prior to the start of the project, the project manager must ensure that the development environment is stable, suitable, and appropriate for the project team's use. The development environment is the framework that provides the optimal opportunity for success.

BENEFITS OF THE DEVELOPMENT ENVIRONMENT

The development environment is part of the development organization's overall success strategy and must be structured to:

- Support IT's mission to align technology solutions with business requirements;
- Maintain underlying technologies; and
- Be flexible to the changing characteristics of technology.

The infrastructure forms the foundation for a development team's project culture. It provides the team with discipline and fosters the culture that management requires to be effective. The mechanisms for communication, process, and deliverables are organized by the framework formed by the infrastructure. Its form and definition must be structured enough to withstand the demands placed upon it. The more care and attention committed to planning and managing the infrastructure, the more opportunity there is to realize accurate expectations and project success.

The development environment, when correctly used by the project team, will provide the following benefits:

■ Provide a clear sense of the project vision and purpose;

■ Communicate the progress, issues, and roles within the development team;

■ Communicate issues, requirements, and feedback to the end-user community;

■ Establish and enforce meaningful, concise, and modifiable standards; and

■ Provide the team with the items necessary to support interdependence, consistency, and efficiency.

IDENTIFYING THE NECESSARY COMPONENTS

Considerations

It is critical to recognize the underlying mission of the IT organization in order to select the correct development environment toolset.

■ Is the group's primary focus to manage the integration of vendor solutions into existing technology?

or

■ Is the development team empowered to build solutions that are unique and primarily internally driven?

Organizations that are committed to replacing legacy systems with integrated packaged solutions require a different infrastructure than a development shop committed to building custom applications. The tools, standards, and techniques for package selection and implementation projects are different from those needed for custom development. For example, more robust development tools are needed for custom development projects. Package integration projects require detailed standards that address interface requirements, naming conventions, and integration techniques.

The business environment also impacts the components of the development environment. Solutions that are to be placed in a changing, dynamic, business environment require a far different approach than business applications that will seldom require functional changes. For example, a marketing application will typically require more functional modifications that an accounting systems' general ledger.

Configurations

The development environment is more than just development tools used by the programming team. It must support all layers illustrated in Figure 6–1 through standards, tools, techniques, templates, and services. If a suitable testing tool is provided as part of the toolset, but there is no standard desktop configuration for testing, then the tool is of minimal benefit. Testing results become dependent on differences in hardware and software.

Therefore, the development environment must first address the standard configurations that will be used by the development team. They must identify what hardware, software, communications, and networking software and tools will be used by the team. The development configurations may be different than the application's deployment configurations. For example, the development team may use Windows 95, but the end-users are an installed Macintosh base.

The development environment configurations were outlined in the technology strategy. The project manager must verify that the configurations are still appropriate for the team. The most influential factors in selecting a development platform include:

- Existing development tools
- Development platforms of packaged solutions that will be integrated

Client Platform: Hardware, operating system software
Presentation Services: Window management, printing, multimedia software & hardware
Application Software: Executable code, business logic
Network: Hardware & software (operating, communications, support)
Middleware: Application communication & distribution software
Server Platform: Hardware, operating system software
Database: DBMS, data management software

FIGURE 6–1. Development environment.

■ Evaluation of tools for their compatibility with a wide range of technologies often referred to as an "Open System" compliant

■ Market position of the potential tools

Toolset

The project manager must also review the toolset that will be used throughout the development process. The toolset consists of tools, standards, templates, and services.

The toolset should include, at a minimum:

- Methodology repository containing standard procedures and form templates
- Development standards, including naming, programming, testing, and communications
- Prototype design tools
- Physical and logical data analysis tools
- Source code management and version control
- GUI and database testing tools
- Project control and management software
- Time management software
- Groupware, e-mail, or other communications software
- Object repository and corresponding libraries

A client/server solution cannot be built without a commitment to a GUI development tool and a relational database solution. These two components must be selected before an assessment of the infrastructure can be completed. If the development tool and database standard are in place, the decisions relative to making the tools selections, listed above, will be less challenging. Try to limit the number of development tools and relational databases. The IT organization that can focus its expertise on one development tool and one database has significant leverage with resources and tools choices.

SELECTING THE RIGHT TOOLS

There is no more controversial, dynamic, or difficult task than the process of selecting the "right" tools. Everyone has an opinion. Some organizations are committed to building their own suite of tools that will become their homegrown toolset; other organizations will acquire a collection of commercial products and adapt them to their needs. The following sections provide some guidelines for evaluating products and selecting components of the development environment.

General Considerations

Assess the organization's needs, timeline, and budgets. Determine whether a commercial product will be purchased or if the solution will be internally developed. The considerations for evaluating a purchased solution are the same as for an internally constructed solution.

Be very careful not to select tools that will limit available technical resources to a small and elite group. For example, when evaluating a relational database, at a minimum, the choices must be SQL capable. SQL has become the standard database query language for the corporate environment.

Select components of the toolset based on the following priorities:

- Market share of the provider
- Life cycle of the product relative to "state of the art"
- Integration tool's hardware platform, operating system, and network operating system platform
- Business timelines to implement the new technology
- Skills inventory of existing and marketplace resources

Develop a weighted scale that takes into account the candidate product and its strengths relative to these priorities. When this book was in its initial writing, Sun's Java and Microsoft's Active X would not have appeared on the list of viable technologies that would be considered to meet development needs. Tools change quickly and many professional IT managers have begun the search for new employment as the result of poor decision making.

Assess the training available with the product, the trainer quality, and the training materials. Consider the costs of training when determining the costs of the product. If the product is internally assembled, the cost to build and deliver training will be quite different than that acquired from an outside vendor.

Evaluate the consulting services offered by the vendor to assist with the implementation. Determine the types and costs of available long-term support services. Identify, up-front, the support and maintenance fees. Be sure to understand how the product is licensed—site, seat, concurrent usage, etc.

If time allows, pilot the product of choice on one project before rolling it out to the entire development organization. Train all the members of the pilot project team. At the conclusion of each stage of the pilot project, review the items that should be customized or changed before the product is used by the full organization.

When selecting a product, be careful of falling into the "analysis-paralysis" trap. An IT organization can spend years selecting, customizing, training, and rolling-out the best toolset. At some point, all products look good. At that point, pick one and go with it.

Methodology Selection

The methodology must support maintenance projects, package selection and implementation efforts, and custom development. Each stage of development will have unique deliverables. The methodology must support the production of each deliverable and track its progress. Refer to *Chapter 5: Following the Right Process* for a list of the key deliverables for each stage. Evaluate the following areas when selecting a methodology for the development environment:

Appropriateness
  ■ Does it support the development approaches you will follow?

■ Is it geared towards client/server development, or focused on host-based applications? How are the critical client/server issues addressed?

■ What roles are used throughout the project?

■ What level of guidance is provided by the methodology? Does the methodology provide sufficient guidance for development techniques, such as joint application design?

■ Is sufficient direction given for completing the deliverables? Are sample deliverables provided?

■ Is it within your budget?

Flexibility

■ Does the methodology provide insights into techniques related to using the selected development tools?

■ How does the methodology fit with our corporate culture? Is it close to the process we currently follow? Is the terminology clear? Is the content well written? Does it provide enough information? Too much information? Are examples provided with the techniques?

■ How can the methodology content, deliverables, and techniques be customized? Can tasks be modified, deleted, or added? Can roles be modified?

■ How are the deliverables made available for use? Do they have to be re-created in order to have them available electronically? Can content be printed or otherwise exported?

■ Is the content delivered on-line, in binders, or both? If the content is delivered via on-line help, is the original document provided? What tools are used to create the help file? Does the organization currently have those skills?

Project management aspects

■ What level of support is given to the project manager? Are estimating parameters provided? Are there specific deliverables for the project manager?

- What management roles are recognized? How are end-users involved?

- What project management tool functions are provided with the methodology? Can a task list be created? Can it be exported easily to other project management tools? Is the product worth the cost? What are the productivity expectations?

Standards

The selection of standards should be a less challenging effort because the marketplace has fewer standards products available. Many times, the standards will be internally developed.

The areas evaluated when selecting a methodology should also be evaluated for standards. When developing standards internally, focus on making them as user-friendly as possible.

Pursue the standards selection tasks based on a recognition of the areas within the technology mix where industry guidelines have been established. For example, platform-specific standards for GUI look, feel, and controls are publicly available and widely distributed.

Other Infrastructure Tools

The development software should be used to provide prototyping views. Project management and resource management tools should be industry leaders. All other tools, other than communications, are dependent on specific development and database platforms. These include data analysis for physical database design, source code management, version control, and testing software.

The concept of using groupware tools as the key communications vehicle is important to understand clearly. Groupware should be implemented within the team to act as an audit trail of development activity and related conversations.

Project managers can cut and paste documents, reports, screen shots, and related documents so that the historical views for this project and future projects will be assembled in a multimedia format. The ability to build an archival view of a projects development history will bring significant value to future projects.

MAINTAINING THE DEVELOPMENT ENVIRONMENT

The development environment should be owned by the infrastructure team. The maintenance and evolution of the development environment is not a project function. The effort must be done at a central level in order to achieve the benefits described earlier.

Each project must be empowered to apply the infrastructure process and tools. Each project must act as a quality feedback mechanism to insure that the infrastructure remains continuously improved. This can be accomplished by assigning a revolving team to continually assess the components of the development environment, gather feedback, and provide suggestions for improvements. The team should consist of people from the business liaison, consulting, and development teams. They must put into place a mechanism to retrieve feedback from project members at the conclusion of each project stage.

SUMMARY

The development environment provides discipline and structure and requires a clear understanding of the complexity of client/server projects. Development team members need tools, templates, and standards to properly and efficiently complete their tasks. Standards, such as GUI design and testing, will greatly increase the quality of the applications delivered to customers. An effective investment in the development environment will lower the training, maintenance, and support costs over the life of the application.

CHAPTER 7

MANAGING CHAOS

Chaos:
A condition or place of great disorder or confusion

Manage:
To exert control over

Client/server development projects are described by most participants as chaos. There are a multitude of tasks happening—software developers spinning off in their own directions, new issues arising every moment, new releases of technical components, changing requirements—the list goes on and on. Most experienced developers will tell you that, miraculously, out of chaos can come the desired end-result. Well, guess what? The miracle is usually the project manager. The project manager must control the chaos and create a successful application.

The very nature of software development resembles chaos. There are so many varied activities occurring at the same time that there is always some level of disorder and confusion. No matter how detailed the project plans, there is always something not going according to plan. (An argument some project managers use to avoid planning altogether!)

It has been reported that more than 50 percent of client/server projects are "killed" before they ever get implemented. If we did an autopsy on these projects, we would find that management issues contribute far more to project failure than choosing the wrong toolsets. The key to staying above the chaos will always be communication within the team. The project manager must find key team members who can maintain a pulse of the project's progress. Without such personnel, projects will fail over and over again.

In the book *The Inner Game of Tennis,* Tim Gallway presents a focusing technique named "Bounce, Hit."[1] The technique's purpose is to provide the player with a place to put his or her concentration while learning proceeds despite his or her lack of experience. The player focuses on the ball hitting the ground and the sound of the racquet making contact. Like the tennis player, the project manager must find a place to concentrate within the whirlwind of activity that surrounds each and every project.

To remain consistent and stable, the project manager must focus on the factors unique to client/server development efforts and which contribute to the chaos:

[1]Gallway, W. Timothy. *The Inner Game of Tennis.* New York, NY: Random House, 1974.

■ Iteration and overlap in the development process
■ Complexity of technology components

ITERATION AND OVERLAP

A good client/server development methodology does not follow a phased approach; instead, iteration in development of deliverables and overlap between stages is encouraged. A phased, or waterfall, development approach is one where each major segment of work, or stage, is completed before the next stage is begun. This type of approach does not encourage repetition between tasks—once a task is complete, there is no opportunity to review or refine. Sign-off is required at the end of each stage. This sign-off basically says that "This work is done, there's no going back. Let's move to the next stage." For example, all the requirements have been gathered (allegedly) and now we can move to design. It is unrealistic to think that all information can be gathered and accurately understood in one pass, especially for client/server development.

The methodology used for client/server development must incorporate iteration and overlap. Iteration means that tasks are repeated to refine information and deliverables. Overlap refers to using a development approach that is non-phased. Multiple stages are conducted simultaneously. This type of approach recognizes that there is great synergy to be gained from doing tasks concurrently. For example, requirements are gathered and a level of design is simultaneously completed to verify the requirements.

Iteration

The term "iteration" causes most developers and managers to think of Rapid Application Development (RAD) or rapid prototyping methodologies. In these approaches, functionality is prototyped, reviewed, enhanced, reviewed, etc. Some methodologies are based purely on this continual iteration and discovery process. This approach is certainly appropriate for discovering and analyzing requirements, especially for new business functions or technologies. In our experience, rapid prototyping is best used as a technique to discover and refine requirements and the application's design.

It is dangerous, however, to use this approach to fully build and implement applications. The biggest danger is that the application is not thoroughly designed for the long-term. Re-use principles are not followed. Maintenance and adding functionality becomes a nightmare, pure and simple.

Stick with what works

Example—Software Development Company

A new company was building a new software product using a rapid prototyping approach. This was to be a product for the commercial market and the designers weren't sure exactly how the functionality would be implemented. The product needed to have a unique "angle" to differentiate itself in the marketplace.

Document every move you make

Throughout the development process, the database architecture was continually modified. Also, several windows were created that were very similar in functionality. Finally, because of the speed with which things were created, no documentation was done on the product, which was developed primarily by contractors.

learn from your past. travel in a forward approach.

After the initial release, complaints came in about performance when large amounts of data were entered. The similar windows encountered different bugs and did not act consistently as was expected. When it came time to develop the second release of the product, there was nothing to which to refer. Also, it turns out that the similar windows were not built as reusable objects, but as discrete pieces of code. In the long run, the company decided it was easier to "toss out" major portions of the database design and corresponding code, and re-design and build it.

Iteration in the development process is more than rapid prototyping; it occurs throughout the entire development process. Iteration refers to the *refinement* of information in deliverables, such as requirements lists, end-user profiles, object

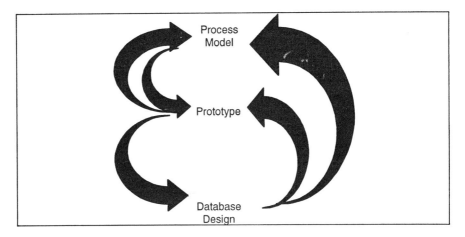

FIGURE 7–1.   Iteration between deliverables.

models, data models, prototypes, module designs, and test cases. In other words, any deliverable can be completed and then updated in light of new information gathered or understood during the completion of other deliverables. Iteration means changing the mind set of "We can't do that because it conflicts with the other deliverable and we need sign-off on it." Iteration means asking the question, "What impact on other deliverables does this new understanding have?" Figure 7–1 illustrates how iteration between deliverables occurs.

Overlap

Overlap in the development process goes hand-in-hand with iteration. Overlap refers to the timing of stages and tasks in the development process. Overlap provides synergy and fits in perfectly with the concept of iteration. A small amount of overlap occurs informally, but the project manager must formalize and enlarge the amount to improve the product developed.

Overlap is beneficial to the project because it enhances the discovery process. For example, as interviews are completed to gather requirements, the various analysis models can be started at a high-level and filled in with the known details. Some design work can be started, including the development of a prototype of critical functions. Questions from the initial analysis of the requirements can be answered as the requirements are gathered. Traditionally, this level of discovery is made during analysis, after the requirements have been "signed off." Then, customers and the development team must re-negotiate the project scope. No wonder customers are dissatisfied with the applications they eventually receive!

Another benefit of incorporating overlap into the project schedules is that testing occurs sooner. As the project moves along, critical windows are built and tested. Feedback can be incorporated into other designs before they are built. Traditionally, this level of feedback is provided during a testing phase, after all the modules have been designed and tested. Changes, if they are accepted, are sweeping and have a large impact on the work already completed.

Figure 7–2 illustrates how overlap between stages can be incorporated into the project schedule.

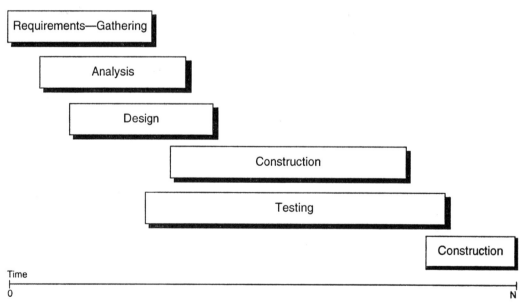

FIGURE 7–2.   Impact of overlap on the development process.

When the diagram in Figure 7–2 is broken down into more detail, as in Figure 7–3, it shows the relative amount of work that is done in each stage at specific points in time. With the exception of requirements gathering and implementation, each stage follows a "bell-curve" of effort. A small amount of design is completed during requirements gathering. Then, as effort in that area winds down, the effort shifts to design, with some effort expended in coding and testing. Figure 7–3 illustrates how the amount of effort spent on each phase changes throughout the project.

Impact

Done correctly, iteration and overlap add quality to the project, ultimately shortening the development time and cost. This occurs because more information is gathered and understood

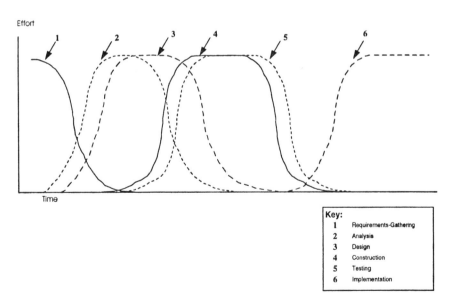

FIGURE 7–3. Effort expended during each stage.

earlier in the development cycle, where there is less impact (and it is less costly).

Think about your last project—isn't a lot of redesign done during the latter stages of testing? That's because the information wasn't fully understood during requirements-gathering. We are used to iteration and overlap between the coding and testing stages, but not used to it between earlier stages of the project. When iteration and overlap occurs in the earlier stages of the project, the end-result is better.

It is even more critical to incorporate iteration and overlap in a client/server project because there is more information to gather and understand. The requirements are different and more complex; the architecture impacts the application design; the end-user doesn't always understand the capabilities the application can give them. Iteration and overlap aid the discovery process and provide the opportunity to correct small mistakes before they become huge mistakes.

Traditionally, the project manager encounters great pressure to begin coding to produce something tangible for the end-user to see. This pressure is even greater on client/server development projects—development tools can quickly create portions of the graphical user interface for the end-user to see. This encourages a rush to complete the analysis and move on. As a result, issues are ignored or quickly settled. During testing, though, they reappear and demand resolution. Incorporating iteration and overlap into the development process slows this rush and delivers positive results.

Scheduling Projects with Iteration and Overlap

Iteration and overlap can add a level of disorder to a project. Iteration tends to drive the project manager crazy.

- Is the task complete or not?
- Is the deliverable done or not?
- Did the end-user approve this yet?

■ What does this look like on a Gantt chart?

■ How do I determine the true status of my project?

The best way to schedule projects which incorporate iteration and overlap, is to break tasks down into smaller tasks. Tasks associated with each version of a deliverable are the ideal tasks to schedule, assign resources, and manage. Granted, this approach creates significantly more tasks to enter, report on, and maintain, but this provides a more realistic approach of the project's schedule and progress.

For example, instead of having one task, "Create Interface Navigation Model," that takes many weeks to complete, have multiple shorter tasks. The tasks would be associated with each version of the model. Refer to Table 7–1 for a sample work plan.

TABLE 7–1.   SAMPLE WORK PLAN

Task	Hours	Duration	Required Role
Create Dialogue Navigation Model—Version 1	40 hours	8 days	Interface Designer
Review Dialogue Navigation Model—Version 1	8 hours	2 days	Interface Architect
Create Dialogue Navigation Model—Version 2	30 hours	6 days	Interface Designer
Review Dialogue Navigation Model—Version 2	8 hours	1 day	Interface Architect Business Specialist
Create Dialogue Navigation Model—Version 3	20 hours	5 days	Interface Designer
Review Dialogue Navigation Model—Version 3	4 hours	1 day	Interface Architect Business Specialist
Complete Final Modifications	4 hours	1 day	Interface Designer
Review & Approve Final Model	4 hours	1 day	Interface Architect Business Specialist

This scheduling approach also addresses the complications of scheduling overlap. It creates more realistic task dependencies. Using larger tasks, such as "Create Interface Navigation Model," creates more complicated dependencies. The next task, "Design Primary Windows," would start when "Create Interface Navigation Model" is 65 percent done. This becomes difficult to schedule, communicate, and manage.

Breaking down both tasks creates a schedule with more realistic task dependencies. The task "Design Primary Windows—Version 1" is started when the task, "Review Interface Navigation Model—Version 2," is finished.

Scheduling a project with iteration and overlap requires a more detailed project plan. This comes with the cost of additional management and administrative overhead. The benefit, however, is an easier-to-understand project plan that increases communication with the project team, the end-users, and upper management.

Success Factors

There are many benefits to be gained from incorporating iteration and overlap into your development process. The cost is an increase in the chaos. But as the title of this chapter suggests, chaos can be managed. Follow these critical success factors when managing a client/server project that incorporates overlap and iteration:

- Understand the development process and how information flows from one deliverable to another. This will help you identify the deliverables that need refinement, based on new or changing information.
- Emphasize the completion of deliverables, not tasks. The focus of the project should be gathering and understanding all the necessary information, not just checking off completed tasks.

■ Base the project schedule on versions of deliverables. Some critical deliverables, such as analysis models, may require four or five versions until they are complete. Relate tasks to specific versions of critical deliverables.

■ Follow the 80/20 rule—80 percent of the information will be gathered during the first several iterations; this takes about 20 percent of the total time. The remaining 80 percent of the time is required to refine and gather the remaining 20 percent of the information.

■ Timebox—Some deliverables, namely prototypes, can be refined forever, with ever diminishing returns. Limit the number of iterations and the time spent developing each iteration.

■ Keep the team of critical roles to ten full-time equivalents (FTEs) or less. As the team size increases, more overhead must be spent on communication. If the project is large enough to require multiple teams, assign a full-time team-leader to each. The team leader's responsibility is to communicate changes and issues between teams.

■ Communicate—Informal communication between team members, including the end-users, is critical to the success of any client/server development effort.

COMPLEXITY OF TECHNOLOGY COMPONENTS

Client/server projects have many technical aspects. A client/server application consists, many times, of new technologies implemented in numerous interrelated components. Technology components include:

■ Software development tools and environments
■ Desktop hardware for development
■ Desktop and laptop hardware for deployment
■ Operating system platforms

- Server hardware for development and deployment
- Database environments and utilities
- Middleware
- WAN, LAN, and Web
- Network operating environments

The sheer volume of technical components and the rapid changes to available products increases the project's complexity and associated level of chaos. In the past, the project manager was not required to understand and manage the technical details. Mainframe technology was proven and stable, and the project team was experienced in those areas.

Today, the project manager must have a clear understanding of the strengths, weaknesses, and capacity of the technology that is targeted for the project's development and deployment environment in order to:

- Build project plans that include the necessary technical tasks and the correct amount of time to complete them;
- Allocate the right resources to technical tasks;
- Bring in qualified outside resources;
- Respond to the impact of a change in one technical component on other components and the project schedule, as a whole;
- Support the technical architect in decisions in defining the architecture and any trade-offs between technical functionality, costs, performance, or reliability;
- Understand "vendor-speak" and determine the real costs and benefits; and
- Ensure that the project team has the appropriate tools and support.

The project manager must still rely on the technical expertise of the project team. When completing the first client/server projects, however, the expertise is not as deep as it was on mainframe or PC applications. Nor is it as wide—the expertise may be limited to a newly hired technical architect and several technical analysts.

Success Factors

Today's reality is that client/server development requires a project manager that is comfortable with technology. The project will not be successful if the project manager is not willing and able to address the technical issues that invariably arise. The project manager must make it a priority to understand the technologies selected for the project by attending training and seminars, reading the trade journals, and asking questions of the technical staff.

This need for technical literacy is an ongoing task for the project manager. Specific to each project, however, there are two tasks that must be completed in order to improve the chances of success in managing the project's chaos:

- Create a conceptual description of the application's deployment environment.
- Verify that the development environment, or infrastructure, is aligned with the deployment environment.

During initial client/server projects, there is a tendency to treat the constraints of the deployment environment as an "after-the-project" concern. As a result, many mission-critical applications have been built that are effective for departmental deployment, but cannot withstand the rigors of today's remote computing or the demands of enterprise and Internet computing.

Today's client/server solutions reside on desktops that are loaded with a wide variety of applications. It is unrealistic to assume that the deployed application is the only application running on the desktop. Do not base the desktop (client) configuration requirements solely on the demands of the deployed application. The *minimum* requirements for client configuration must assume that the operating and network environment, the client application, and two productivity tools are operating simultaneously. To treat the deployment environment as an afterthought will only create project chaos.

Prior to the start of the project, the conceptual requirements of the deployment environment must be known. This conceptual description provides the team with a well-defined explanation of the demands that will be placed upon the deployed system. This knowledge then allows the project manager to staff the project with people skilled in the technologies that will be used. It also provides the project manager with a list of technologies that must be understood.

Knowledge of the deployment environment also provides the basic requirements for the development infrastructure. The tools and associated technologies selected to build the application must have the capacity to support the deployment environment.

There is a tendency within development teams to select tools that are based on the developers' skills rather than the tools' strengths. This approach can lead to significant project constraints. The project manager must find a balance between the time constraints of the project, the complexity of the application, the skills inventory, and the tools marketplace. Refer to *Chapter 6: Establishing the Development Infrastructure* for a more detailed discussion.

SUMMARY

There is a clear difference between "management by chaos" and managing the chaos of a client/server project. The factors that contribute to the chaos include:

- Iteration and overlap in the development process
- Complexity of technology components

We acknowledge that the demands of a client/server project can spin out of control. The successful project leader will manage people, process, technology, and tools to combat the natural project tendency toward chaos. A management style that is not organized and structured will be challenged to succeed in this environment.

CHAPTER 8

KNOWING THE END-RESULT

Scope:
The area covered by a given activity or subject

One reason that over 50 percent of all development efforts fail is the lack of a properly defined application scope. Knowing the scope may be the most difficult part of any project, and has been a constant challenge to project managers. This challenge is no less significant for client/server projects. In fact, many development managers have found it more difficult to scope a client/server application because of the additional technical areas that require definition.

Project teams sometimes feel that defining an application's scope simply involves building a comprehensive list of requirements based on interviews with the end-users and their management. This is really just a start. An application's scope consists of a complete definition of the following items:

- Application functions
- Market for the application
- End-user profiles
- Application priorities

The functionality required by the application provides the basis for the application's scope. The functions give the information about "What the application must do." This is critical, but the scope definition must also answer the question of "For whom does the application do this?" The market for the application and the end-user profile clearly define the audience for the application.

These items are tightly integrated and cannot be analyzed apart from one another. For example, you cannot really understand the end-user profile if you haven't first determined if the application will be used internally or sold to an outside market. The application's priorities (such as performance or usability) cannot be accurately determined without first understanding who the end-users are and what they expect from the application.

The process and techniques for gathering requirements will be discussed in later chapters. This chapter focuses on defining the application's scope in terms of its functions, market, end-user profiles, and priorities.

FUNCTIONS—DEFINING APPLICATIONS VERSUS DEFINING PROJECTS

People tend to "wear blinders" while defining an application. They immediately think of what can be delivered within the parameters of a specific project, instead of what the total application should be: "We have 12 months and we can get x, y, and z functions done and that's it." In other words, they define the *project* and not the *application*. There is a big difference, especially in complex client/server applications.

Instead of focusing on the entire application, a project should focus on delivering a *release* of the application. An application release is a discrete set of new or improved functionality that provides specific benefits. A release should be completed and delivered within a six to 12-month timeframe. It is not good project management practice to have client/server development projects last for more than 12 months (and that's on the long side!). There are too many changes in that amount of time, both functionally and technically.

Commercial software builders provide a good example of release scoping. They provide the core functionality in the first release. The next releases add on to that functionality and provide more and more to the end-users. The most effective approach for defining an application is to gather a "wish list" of the functionality the end-users need and want. This list should then be analyzed and used to define specific application releases.

The following questions can help you group functions into releases:

■ What functions are essential?
■ What functions build on other functions?

■ What functions provide the most immediate benefits?

■ What functions have the most synergy between them?

■ What is the approximate cost for providing this set of functionality, in terms of time and resources?

■ What is the approximate cost for not providing this set of functionality, in terms of lost benefits and opportunity costs?

■ What is the cost of adding other functionality in later releases, in terms of development time and resources?

Knowing all the desired functions helps the development team build the application in a modular, reusable, easily added-onto fashion. From an expectation management perspective, it is important to not *promise* functionality when initially gathering information about the application. It is also important to not *eliminate* functions, consciously or unconsciously.

Another obstacle that IT organizations face is the historical experiences end-users have with the development process. End-users believe, and rightly so, that if they do not ask for all functionality now, they will never see it. Because of this perspective, upper management must support the application release approach. This support, along with communicating the scope and schedule to end-users, will begin to ease their concerns.

THE MARKET FOR THE APPLICATION

Defining the marketplace for the application is critical for defining the application's scope, as well as the release schedule. The most important question every member of the project team must be able to answer is: "Who will be using this application?"

Starting at the highest level, you need to determine whether the application will be used by people in your organization or used by people external to your organization (the commercial market). There is also a growing trend in which an application is developed primarily for internal use and is then sold on a limited basis to other companies within the industry. The market for the application greatly influences many areas of the development process. These areas are listed in Table 8–1.

Internal Use

Developing an application solely for internal use provides its own set of challenges, the largest being the corporate culture (also known as politics). However, there is typically less variability and more "knowns" than when developing an application for the commercial market.

When a client/server application is developed for internal use, the development team has more access to the end-users

TABLE 8–1. AREAS INFLUENCED BY THE APPLICATION MARKET

- Access to end-users: interviewing, review sessions, and testing sessions
- Knowledge of the end-user
- Number of end-users
- Categories of end-users
- Overall application priorities
- Functional requirements
- Technical platform requirements
- Security requirements
- Sources for requirements
- Amount of customization needed
- Ease of use, installation and maintenance
- Maintenance, distribution, and support priorities
- Release and phasing strategies
- Documentation and training approaches
- Development approach used to build the application
- Project management techniques
- Techniques for requirements-gathering, prototyping, testing, distribution

and some of the end-users are part of the project team. In this situation, the number of end-users is more easily determined and there are a limited number of end-user categories. The end-users typically have the same overall set of priorities for the application and their functional and technical requirements are somewhat common.

Requirements are gathered from the actual end-users, through study of the existing application, and from the project team member's knowledge of the company's business functions. Distribution, installation, training, and access to documentation can be controlled and sometimes even completed by the development team. Releases and project phases are scheduled to coincide with corporate milestones. The application can be developed using either a custom or packaged approach; the development approach is determined primarily by the functionality required in the application.

Commercial Market

Developing an application for the external, or commercial, market has its own challenges. The biggest challenge is to determine what market is being targeted by the application.

The most tempting, and worst choice, is to try to be all things to all people. Developing software requires many trade-offs, including the one between functionality, performance, and price. It is difficult, if not impossible, to create a product that provides the best in functionality and performance, without creating massive technical requirements. (This is to say nothing about training and documentation requirements, or price!)

In developing software for the commercial market, it is much better to deliver a smaller amount of functionality that performs well and without errors. Obviously, there has to be enough functionality to entice people to buy the product. Future releases provide the opportunity to add functionality.

Determining the target market for the application is difficult because there is no easy access to the end-users. Market research, marketing experts, and beta groups substitute for access to the actual end-users. Many assumptions have to be made about the end-user categories, numbers, and application priorities. However, once this information is established, it typically does not change. Functionality must also be determined through market research, marketing experts, and beta groups. Studying the competition is also an excellent way to identify requirements, especially the "must-have" requirements.

The technical platform requirements must also be determined through the same mechanisms as the functional requirements.

- What technical platforms will be supported?
- What do most of our potential customers already have?
- What versions of what operating systems?
- What is the future direction of the technical platforms?

As more and more client/server applications are delivered, the number of potential technical platform combinations greatly increases. Because of the variability in end-users and technical environments, commercial applications need to provide the ability for the customer to modify and customize the installation parameters during roll-out. This ability can be built into the software or it can be delivered through the use of consultants. The roll-out, documentation, and training strategies also influence the customization approach used.

THE END-USER PROFILE

After defining the market for the application, the next important scoping component is the detailed profile, or description, of the end-user. As any marketing wizard will tell you, the most important thing to know before trying to build and sell a product is to know the customer. That concept is just as important to the project manager trying to build and sell a software product.

In today's reality, the project manager is the primary marketing agent for the project, responsible for building excitement and acceptance of the new application. This role is in addition to the responsibilities of ensuring that funds exist, the right people are available, and the project is progressing in an orderly fashion. Unfortunately, with all these other pressures, the knowledge of the end-user usually is assumed or simplified. Mistakes in this basic, crucial information can be devastating to the success of a project.

Thorough knowledge of the end-user is needed for the success of all aspects of a client/server project. Requirements cannot be gathered accurately without knowing all the various categories of end-users and how they differ. Obviously, design of the application will be inaccurate and incomplete if the end-user's priorities and abilities are not understood. How can a good GUI be designed without knowing the educational level, native language, and computer literacy of each end-user category? Or without knowing how they will do their job? The task of testing an application even benefits from a thorough knowledge of the end-user because testers can be selected who are representative of each end-user category.

Capture information about the end-users in an End-User Profile. One profile should be created for each category of end-user. The profile contains all the information about the end-users of the software product. The information is derived from interviews with management, end-users, and human resources, as well as the development team's knowledge of the end-user and the business environment.

Table 8-2 contains some of the questions you must answer to complete the End-User Profile.

As this list suggests, a complete profile cannot be given by a single statement—nor can it be gathered in a few hours. The End-User Profile is completed during the requirements-gathering stage of the project and continually refined. At a minimum, each question must briefly be answered while scoping the proj-

TABLE 8–2.   INFORMATION NEEDED FOR THE END-USER PROFILE

- Who are they? What are their job titles?
- What do they do? What is their job description?
- How do they do their job?
- How will this application help them?
- What are their expectations of the application, both positive and negative? What problems do they expect it to solve? What benefits do they expect it to provide? What are the priorities of the application from their perspective?
- How will this application change their jobs or work environment?
- In their opinion, what is the most important feature of the application?
- What is their educational level?
- What is their native language?
- What is their age? Are they visually impaired? Physically impaired? Hearing impaired?
- What is their experience level with the business domain?
- What other similar business-domain applications have they used? What is their experience level with them? What problems do they expect the new application to solve?
- Are they part of our company or are they in the commercial market? Which division? Which commercial market?
- What business terminology do they use?
- How long have they been in their current position?
- What is their typical technical environment?
- What level of technical ability do they have?
- How many people fit this profile?
- What percent of the total end-user population is supported by this profile?

ect. An understanding of the number of different types of end-users, their abilities, and technical understanding is needed to reliably plan and estimate the project.

As the project progresses, analysis of the End-User Profile is conducted. Additional details are gathered and refined. Remember that the profile is not of an individual end-user, but of a type of end-user. The types of end-users can also be categorized more broadly, based on similarities between them. Data modeling techniques, such as super and sub-classes, and tools can help determine and document the various categories of end-users. Complete an End-User Category Summary for each category. Document the differentiating factors of the category and describe the overall characteristics. Then complete a detailed End-User Profile for the category. Any set of values on the End-User Profile can be used to categorize the profiles, but the following areas are especially useful:

- Use of the application (strategic vs. tactical, business vs. technical)
- Work team (executive vs. management vs. clerical)
- Education level
- Technical proficiency
- Market (in-house vs. commercial)

For the Information Technology person, information about the end-user can be very enlightening, as well as helpful. Unfortunately, many client/server projects do not spend enough time in this area and the results are disastrous.

Example—Manufacturing Company

The company was building a client/server system for their order-processing function. There were several different end-user groups that would use the system; there were over 15 different end-user profiles. Analysis was done on the technical platforms in use in the company and the decision was made to build the application to run in an OS/2 environment. The group doing data-entry of the orders would be converted from DOS, character-based applications to OS/2, GUI applications. The project progressed through the design stage. Finally, the project team had built several prototypes and were ready to conduct usability tests. During the tests, they discovered that the data-entry group consisted of union employees. Their pay rate was based in part by the technical skills required of them. Converting to an OS/2, GUI application raised their labor costs over 25 percent! Fortunately, the project team was able to change the technical implementation without significant costs, but not without delaying the application's implementation.

If the profile of the end-users is unclear or incomplete, serious problems can occur. Also, it is difficult to know what the priorities for the application are, what requirements-gathering techniques are most appropriate, or if a suitable application already exists in the marketplace.

APPLICATION PRIORITIES

The market definition and, obviously, the end-user profile relate to the end-users of the application. Application priorities, the next component of the application's scope, relate to the application itself. Application priorities are the items that directly impact the application's scope. They are an overall influencing factor—they affect all aspects of the application's lifecycle. The application priorities influence decisions that impact the application in the short and long-term. For example, two application priorities are budget and performance. If meeting a set budget is a high priority, then decisions regarding performance improvements will be based more on budget than on the benefits of the improvements.

The priorities for an application are also the factors by which the end-users determine if it is a quality application. There are many definitions of quality. For purposes of this book, a quality application is defined simply as an application that does what it needs to do, at the levels at which it is required—no more, no less. Therefore, to build a quality application, you must be able to determine what the application must do and what its priorities are.

Application priorities are defined during the requirements-gathering process. Seldom, if ever, will an application have just one priority. "Make the application as reusable as possible, whatever it takes!" More likely, an application has several priorities that the project manager must manage at all times. The priorities for an application guide the project manager in making trade-offs among scope, schedule, and budget throughout the life of the project. Inevitably, trade-offs between these priorities must be made. For example, if the schedule is more important than accuracy, testing may be cut short in order to release the application on its desired date. Or, if a technology should be used (to build technical skills in a project team or for marketing purposes), reusability and functionality may not be as important. Or, if an application release is intended to be a "bug-fix" release, then accuracy is more important than increasing the scope of functionality. On the other hand, if a release is intended to be a functionality upgrade, then scope of functionality may be more important than reusability.

Each major group of people involved with the application's lifecycle may weigh the same priorities differently. They have their own set of priorities and concerns. The development team is concerned with the project's parameters: schedule, bud-

TABLE 8–3.   APPLICATION PRIORITIES: PROJECT PARAMETERS

Priority	Definition
Release scope	The amount of functionality that must be included in the specific release, which is measured partially by the business benefits the release delivers.
Development schedule	The timeline that the project must follow, including a specific release date.
Budget	The amounts of resources, money, and people available for the development of the release.
Risk	The level of risk that is acceptable to management; risks are the items that may incur significant costs or cause project failure.

get, scope, and risks. The end-users are concerned with the functionality and usability of the application. The maintenance and support team is concerned with the scalability and reusability of the application once it is in production.

Tables 8-3 through 8-5 define the application priorities, categorized by the concerns they address.

When clearly understood, application priorities are a powerful project management tool. They can remove some of the

TABLE 8–4.   APPLICATION PRIORITIES: APPLICATION PARAMETERS

Priority	Definition
Scope of functionality	The amount of functionality that must be included in the application, which is measured partially by the business benefits the application delivers.
Accuracy	Functional accuracy, which can be partially measured by the number of errors in the released application.
Usability	The ease of use of the application, which can be partially measured by the amount of training or documentation needed.
Visual appeal	The use of aesthetic elements to entice the user into wanting to use the application (in real estate this is known as "curb appeal").
Performance	The speed, or response time, of the application under normal production conditions.
Availability	The time the application is available for use, which is measured in part by the number of software "crashes" and the amount of time required to repair problems encountered during production.
Use of technology	The implementation of a specific technology in the application.

TABLE 8–5.   APPLICATION PRIORITIES: MAINTENANCE
& SUPPORT CONCERNS

Priority	Definition
Scalability	The ability of the application to grow and adapt over time to changes in the number of end-users, number of transactions processed, and number of technical platforms supported.
Maintainability	The ease of adding new functionality, changing or correcting existing functionality, or transitioning knowledge from the development team to the support team.
Reusability	The ability to use portions of the application's designs, code, executables, training, and documentation in other applications with little or no modifications.
Ease of upgrades	The ability to easily upgrade the production application, measured in part by the number of configuration or database changes required to execute the new release of the application.

"guess-work" in making decisions. They can also help the project team remain focused on what is considered important at the end of the project.

Example—Software Company

The company was building their first software product to be sold on the commercial market. In order to break into the highly competitive market they had chosen, they needed to prove that they were able to produce a quality product. The product needed to be accurate, solid, and stable. Complex functionality was of limited importance because the marketplace did not expect much functionality in the first release of a product. More time and resources were allocated for the testing stage than for other stages of the development cycle. During testing, all requests for changes or additions to functionality were recorded but not immediately implemented. After several stages of testing were completed, stable areas were allowed modest increases in functionality. Areas that were still experiencing software crashes and inaccuracies were not allowed increases in functionality.

As a result of the focus on accuracy and availability, the product did not require a "bug fix" release during its first six months on the marketplace. Also, customers did not experience any data corruption or other major errors when using this first release. The marketplace recognized that the company had produced a quality product.

SUMMARY

The components critical to successfully defining a client/server application are the application functions, the market defined for the application, end-user profiles, and the application's priorities. A solid understanding of these components will better define the application releases and project's scope. Knowing the end-result will help the project team achieve success with their client/server implementation.

PART 3

CLIENT/SERVER SUCCESS TECHNIQUES

HENDERSON, SORRELL

Department	MAKEREA{AC
Badge	2083
ID Number	7-4
Class	1
Rate	1.00

Time Card Report
1/09/99 to 1/15/99

Day	Date	IN	OUT	IN	OUT	Totals	Schedules	
SAT	1/09/99	7:48	13:43			5:55	Unsch.	
MON	1/11/99	10:50	14:57	15:24	20:30	9:10	Unsch.	
TUE	1/12/99	11:03	14:57	15:26	19:44	8:11	Unsch.	
WED	1/13/99	10:13	15:18	15:42	21:13	10:30	Unsch.	
THU	1/14/99	10:58	15:36	15:49	19:51	8:23	Unsch.	
FRI	1/15/99	10:20	16:02	16:18	19:24	8:34	Unsch.	

Pay Designation	Hours	Rate	Dollars
REGULAR	40:00	1.00	40.00
OVERTIME	10:43	1.00	10.72

Department	Hours
MAKEREADY	50:43

1/18/99

CHAPTER 9

DEFINING THE DETAILS

Define:
To state the precise meaning of

Details:
Particulars considered individually and in relation to a whole

Project success depends on many factors, such as effectively and appropriately involving the end-users, and successfully determining the application's functionality. To define the scope of an application successfully, not only must the big picture (functions, marketplace, end-user profiles, and application priorities) be correct, the details also need to be defined accurately. The details of the functionality are the things that make the application great, instead of "just okay."

Details are the exception rules and processing needs. Details are the finer points of the user interface that make it more intuitive. Details are the things that the end-users notice. End-users do not notice (or care about!) the complexity of the architecture or the re-usability of the code. End-users care about the things that make their jobs easier. You may have the most expert Information Technology (IT) professionals on your team, but they will not get all the details right. Only involving the right end-users at the right time will improve your chances of getting the details right. To ensure you are prepared to define the details, you must:

- Understand the need for end-users
- Select the right people as end-users
- Effectively utilize end-users
- Enhance communication with end-users
- Successfully gather requirements from end-users

THE NEED FOR END-USERS

The development team must understand the importance of the end-users' input. There is an age-old war between the IT team and the end-user community. Each side feels the other knows nothing about what they do. There is some truth to that feeling, but the underlying sentiment is dangerous.

There is much debate regarding the level of expertise the development team should have with the end-users' jobs. Should they be able to do their jobs or should they be ignorant/naive about what the end-users do? During the initial stages of the project, the developers do not need to know so much that they are able to complete the end-users' daily tasks. Instead, they must know how to obtain the information from the end-users on how their tasks are completed. Through this exposure, the developer gains knowledge about the tasks, as opposed to developing expertise in completing the tasks. Throughout the project, though, the developers gain deeper knowledge about the tasks in order to design the most appropriate software for the end-users.

Unfortunately, some developers pride themselves on *not* involving the end-users in the project. We have been told repeatedly that "The highest level of developer doesn't need the end-user to build a system." This type of developer thinks they should understand the business sufficiently to identify the requirements and be able to *tell the end-users what they need.* How can someone be an expert in the end-users' job, knowing all the business rules, exception processing, and work flows, and also be an expert in software development? That attitude is deadly to a client/server project and must be eliminated immediately.

The members of the IT organization should strive to attain a level of proficiency in the business environment. They should know the terminology that is used, the primary pieces of information that are required for the essential business processes. They should understand how data flows through the process and what decisions are made along the way. They should also understand the impact that major decisions have upon the work-flow process.

The overall project definitely benefits from having business knowledge on the team, but the adage "a little knowledge is a dangerous thing" is painfully true. Developers with experience in the business domain should never think they can be a *substitute* for the end-user. When end-users are not adequately involved, the results are always insufficient. Functionality is inaccurate or incomplete, data is missed, processes are changed inappropriately, and priorities are misunderstood.

Example—International Training Company

A large international training company was upgrading its training registration system. The end-users of the system were the people responsible for registering participants in specific courses. From a business process perspective, there were very few limitations or constraints. Participants could register for as many courses as they wanted to at one time. The same course could be offered at multiple locations at one time. Unfortunately, the team did not encourage the participation of the end-users after initial scope setting until beta testing. After participating in interviews, the end-users did not participate in any analysis, design, or review sessions! During the beta tests, it became apparent that some of the business rules were not understood by the development team. For example, the database design could not support multiple offerings of the same course, on the same dates, at different locations. When the end-users presented the development team with this problem, the team responded with "Well, just don't offer the same course at different locations at the same time." In other words, change your business process to accommodate our artificial software limitation!

By not involving the end-users throughout the development process, the development team failed to understand the finer points of the business processes and rules. The answer they gave to the end-users is not acceptable. Business processes should not be changed solely to accommodate software limitations.

Our history as information technology professionals is littered with similar (and worse) stories. Traditionally, we don't provide the proper mechanisms for end-users to give their feedback, but we hold them accountable for the end result. No wonder it is difficult to get end-users involved! Who, in their right mind, would want that job?! So how can end-users be involved and effectively used?

SELECTING END-USERS

First, you must determine to whom the term "end-user" applies. Are the end-users the people representing the end-user community on the project? Are the end-users the people who use the completed product? Are the end-users the people who are interviewed to determine requirements?

Yes—the end-users are all of the above. There are different roles that the end-users play in the development process. The end-users are defined as the:

- People who will use the completed product
- Business process experts
- Owners of the application
- Primary sources of information for the application's requirements

It is not practical or beneficial to include all the end-users on the project team. There is also little benefit from interviewing all the people who will use the product for their requirements. The general end-user community characteristics and requirements are documented in the End-User Profiles (refer to *Chapter 8: Knowing the End-Result* for details). Instead of involving the entire end-user community, each project has several people that represent the end-user community. These people are formally part of the project team and fill various project team roles, such as end-user manager and business specialist. The end-user manager helps the team identify the best end-users to provide functional expertise, the best testing candidates, and the best people to resolve functional issues. In a sense, the end-users on the project team are the liaisons between the two communities. They do not replace the end-user community, they act as their communication channel.

A project team should never be denied access to the end-user community if it is needed. Some organizations are not comfortable having an end-user and developer talk directly.

They require that all communication go through intermediaries—the end-users on the project team "appointed" to be the carriers of information between the two groups. Or else, they only allow the managers of the end-user departments to talk to the development team. Either method is dangerous, both in the short-term and the long-term.

For the short-term, there is a danger of requirements and other information becoming distorted. Remember the childhood game of "telephone?" You whispered a simple message into the ear of the person next to you. They then whispered the message to the person next to them, and so on. Finally, the last person repeated the message they heard. The fun came from seeing how disjointed the message became as it went from person to person. In software development, that is not fun, that is failure.

In the long term, the intermediary concept builds the walls between the two communities even higher. Trust and communication deteriorate. The details of the required functionality are lost. To prevent this, the project team needs access to both the managers and the actual end-users of the application.

Many times, a project addresses multiple business communities. When this occurs, the project manager and project sponsor must determine the business areas that require project representation. As a general rule, the most critical and complex business areas should have an end-user as part of the project team. Many times, these people will fill a full-time role on the project, but the size and complexity of the project will dictate the actual time needed. Sometimes, "political pressure" dictates the presence of some end-users to be part of the team. It is important to make sure that all the areas affected by the new application feel that they have adequate representation, either because they have a person on the project team, because the end-users on the team understand their business areas sufficiently enough to ask for the required input, or because they are adequately involved in the requirements-gathering process.

Use the End-User Profiles to identify the areas that need project representation. The profile will tell you what areas are most affected, have the largest population, or are the least positive about the new application.

After the areas that need representation are determined, the individuals who will be part of the project team must be selected. What makes an end-user a good project team member? What set of personality traits and skills are necessary? How do you ensure that you have the best team possible when you don't get to select all of the individuals associated with the team? Traditionally, many projects have been given the less desirable people, the left-overs, the ones who can "be spared." These are not the people who will get the job done.

Example—International Transportation Company

This company was developing a new mission-critical business system. As a result of the new application, many jobs were redefined and some were eliminated. The business areas provided the development team with the required quantity of end-users, but not with the necessary qualifications. The people provided to the team were those who would lose their jobs when the new system rolled out.

The project management team felt they could do fine without quality end-users and accepted the people they were given. The project failed.

The best approach to communicate the importance of the end-user role, and the criticality of staffing it correctly, is to write a "purchase order" to the business area, requesting the specific set of skills you need. Don't get hung up in names and positions on the organization chart. Don't ask for individuals; ask for their characteristics and skills. Treat the position of project team member as the job that it is, not the chore or punishment it is perceived to be. Write a position description to be clear on the requirements. Figure 9–1 provides a sample position description. Notice—the experience and skills required for success are related to interpersonal and decision-making skills, not technical knowledge.

Position Description: End-User Project Team Member

Responsibilities: ■ Act as liaison between business community and development team.
■ Provide input and feedback on business data, events, and processes, and their implementation within the application.
■ Review and approve development deliverables, such as models, prototypes, test cases, and documentation.
■ Fill a specific project role and complete the assigned tasks.
■ Provide accurate and timely status to project management and end-user management.

Experience and Skills Required:

■ Champion of the new application and the overall development process.
■ Knowledgeable of the business' needs.
■ Excellent communication and interpersonal skills.
■ Is influential upwards and peer-to-peer.
■ Can articulate complex processes in a simple fashion.
■ Cannot be swayed easily, but can be convinced.
■ Has the skills necessary to fill the assigned project role.

FIGURE 9–1.   End-user project team member position description.

EFFECTIVELY UTILIZING END-USERS

As the position description states, end-users must fill specific project roles. The overall development effort benefits from having several end-users be full members of the development team filling various roles. Otherwise, end-users just complete tasks in the "input, review/feedback, sign-off" process.

Traditionally, end-users are interviewed for input, are given mounds of documentation to review to "verify" their input was understood correctly, give minimal feedback (because it is too late and will have no impact and the task is in addition to their regular tasks), and then are told to sign-off on the documentation or the project will stop. Not a very pretty process!

This traditional type of involvement is very passive and not very beneficial. It does not encourage ownership and solid decisions. Input must be given over time, not just during the initial steps. Sign-off must indicate agreement on a common understanding, but it also must recognize that the business may change and the system will respond.

As we have seen over the years, this passive involvement ultimately decreases the project's chance for success, short-term and long-term. Incorporating end-users on the project gives them an active role in the development process. They have accountability and the ability to make a difference. Input is given continuously (formally and informally), review and feedback occurs on a more timely basis, and sign-off is less of a political drama.

The roles the end-users fill and the tasks they complete depend on the stage in the development process. Generally speaking, end-users make excellent functional analysts and functional testers. They have the required business background and are not biased by implementation issues. They can identify and describe the business rules and then verify that they were implemented correctly. They can also develop test cases and data, and assess the usability of designs. End-users are excellent subject-matter experts for the application's help, documentation, and training. By involving end-users in active project roles, details will more readily be uncovered.

Table 9–1 depicts the roles and tasks for end-users, relative to the development process. Refer to *Chapter 4: Building the Best Team* for specific details on the responsibilities of each role.

End-users will not be able to meet the responsibilities of their assigned roles without training. They need to become familiar with the terminology and the development process being used on the project and appropriate techniques and tools for their roles. This training should be completed prior to the start of the project, whenever possible. The project manager must make it clear to the end-users and the end-user manager that this training is mandatory. When budgeting the project,

TABLE 9–1.   THE END-USERS' ROLES IN THE PROJECT

Development Stage	Role	Primary Focus
Project Management	End-User Manager	■ Ensure correct end-users are used effectively on the project.
	Team Leader	■ Lead team of functional analysts, testers, or business specialists.
Requirements-Gathering	Business Specialist Functional Analyst	■ Provide information. ■ Gather information.
Analysis	Business Specialist Functional Analyst	■ Review models. ■ Develop models.
Design	Business Specialist	■ Review designs and proto-types. ■ Provide training, documentation, and help content.
	Functional Designer	■ Design test cases.
Testing	Business Specialist	■ Participate in tests. ■ Provide input to design changes.
	Functional Tester	■ Conduct tests and review results.
Implementation	Business Specialist Trainer	■ Attend training. ■ Deliver training.

the project manager should consider this training part of the overall project's cost, just as training on a new tool might be.

ENHANCING COMMUNICATION

Finally, involving the end-users requires strong communication. If the right people are given the right roles and used at the right time in the process, positive results are still not guaranteed. The application's details will not be uncovered in an accurate, timely fashion.

The details are the first thing to be lost when there is ineffective communication. Communication within the IT organization is, generally speaking, effective. Obviously, some organizations are better at communication than others. But as a general rule, the IT personnel within a project team communicate well with one another. They use similar terminology, know and follow the same general processes, sit near each other, and have worked together in the past. Politically, everyone knows their level of influence and the overall "pecking order."

Introducing end-users into the team can disturb this communication. The most common complaint is that end-users are not made to feel part of the team: they are excluded from activities, do not sit near the team, are talked down to, and given tasks to do that do not require interaction with other team members. To get the maximum benefit from involving end-users, these communication barriers must be eliminated.

The most immediate way to improve communication is to adjust the seating area for the team. If people are easy to see, they will become more involved in discussions. If an end-user is sitting next to an analyst, the analyst will ask for more input. Input from end-users becomes an informal event, not requiring meetings and myriads of people. Details will be uncovered and confirmed more quickly. In a meeting structure, the details ("oh by the way, sometimes we have to do ...") are the first things that are forgotten. The implementation of this technique will depend on the space available, the amount of time the end-users spend on the project, and the corporate culture.

Communication also needs to occur with the general end-user community. Some of that responsibility belongs to the end-users themselves. However, to ensure the overall success of the project, the project manager and end-user manager should verify these communications are happening in an effective way. The general end-user community needs to know the overall progress, in as simple a format as possible. They are also interested in seeing how the application will affect them. By exposing the application to more end-users throughout the process, more details will be exposed. The result is a better application and fewer immediate enhancement requests. Buy-in by the general end-user community is also increased, which greatly increases the application's chances for acceptance and success.

Create a bulletin board or newsletter (via "paper," groupware, intranet, or Internet) that is easily accessible and update it with the status of the application. Feature different functions of the application and show samples of windows and reports (when they have been usability tested and are in the best shape). Describe the training and documentation that will be available. Towards the end of the testing stage, have a simple, stable demo available for people to play with.

It is also important to communicate effectively with the end-user management team (the managers responsible for the people who will ultimately use the finished application). They should receive honest status on the project, either in a report or at meetings. Focus on the application's availability, issues related to functionality, and resource requirements. The end-users from the project team and the end-user manager primarily deliver the status, but the project manager is also involved.

Improving communication between the end-user community and the IT organization will have long-lasting benefits, not only for the current project by uncovering the details but, more importantly, for future efforts.

SUCCESSFUL REQUIREMENTS-GATHERING

Effectively involving end-users is one component of defining the details of the application. Successfully gathering requirements is the other critical component. Following a phased development approach, requirements gathering is done only during the first stage of the project; no analysis or design is done at that time.

At the end of this first stage, the end-users sign-off on the requirements and the team moves on to analysis. Guess what – more requirements are uncovered! Then a conflict occurs because the requirements were agreed to by all sides. Now what? Many people try to resolve this problem by changing the meaning of sign-off and by doing more interviewing to get more information. These are valiant attempts, but in reality, this whole process is fundamentally flawed.

In order to successfully gather requirements, you must:

- Follow the appropriate process
- Avoid pitfalls
- Utilize the right techniques

The Process

Requirements-gathering must be done in conjunction with analysis and design, as illustrated in Figure 9–2. This is the only way in which the requirements will be fully uncovered and the details defined.

The timing of this process provides the end-users with something more tangible and comprehensive to review than a list of requirements. They receive analysis models, window

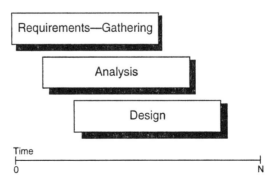

FIGURE 9–2.   The development process: requirements-gathering, analysis, and design.

and report designs, and prototypes of critical functions. These tangible representations of the application provide another opportunity for refining requirements and finding all the details. When end-users see the relationships between data entities, they can further explain other data that is needed, the processes that modify the data, or the exception handling that must be provided. It is during these conversations that the details become apparent. No matter how much interviewing you do, it is not enough. It's just human nature—people think better when given something concrete rather than abstract. As soon as the end-users see the requirements in a less conceptual form, such as a data model, a data flow diagram, or a prototype, they can recall the other parts that are taken for granted. The development team can also identify areas that require more information and clarification.

Pitfalls

A pitfall in using an overlapped approach is losing focus. Requirements-gathering focuses on answering the question "What must the system do? What functions must be supported?" Analysis focuses on the relationships between the functions and identifies all the necessary components. Design determines how the functionality will be implemented. When gathering requirements, it is critical to remain implementation independent. Do not put on "blinders" that block out requirements because of potential difficulty in implementation. This requires discipline, since some design occurs simultaneously with requirements-gathering.

Another pitfall is missing the unstated requirements. When gathering requirements, remember that there are stated requirements and unstated requirements. Your objective is to get the end-users to state *all* of their requirements—leave nothing unstated! Unstated requirements are the items the end-users take for granted and don't articulate: general reporting needs, performance expectations, and basic functionality. From the end-users' perspective, these items may be obvious and do not require stating, they may be things done by habit, or they may be things that they do not know they need to ask for, such as levels of help or error handling reports. Many times, end-users are so close to their business needs and processes, they cannot articulate these details. They also assume that, because it is so important, the functional analyst already knows these requirements.

Think of the last time a new person joined your team. You asked them to write a status report with the following information: tasks completed, tasks to be completed next period, and issues. When you received the report, you realized you forgot to ask for the most critical information: hours spent on each task, estimated hours to completion, and available hours. In almost all cases, unstated requirements are things essential to the system; they cannot be left out and added later. Missing unstated requirements creates scope and schedule chaos for the project manager.

Tips and Techniques

There are many techniques for gathering requirements. When planning a project, look in your "tool kit" of techniques and select the ones most appropriate to your project. Be prepared to modify your selections as the project progresses. Factors that determine which techniques you select include:

- Relationship with the end-user community
- Skills of the development team
- Market for the application (internal or commercial market)
- Development approach and methodology

There are three techniques that must be used on every project. The first is to "Listen, listen, and listen some more." Interviewers should speak very little during an interview; they should be focused on the information the interviewee is pro-

TABLE 9–2.   REQUIREMENTS-GATHERING TECHNIQUES

Technique	Description
Interviewing, General Question & Answer Sessions, Question & Answer within Context of Specific Problem	■ Starts with prepared list of questions, moves to other subjects as necessary ■ Traditional approach ■ Provides general overviews, but with diminishing returns
Surveys, Questionnaires	■ Electronic or paper-based ■ Standard list of questions ■ Mass market "mailing" ■ Typically receive low response
Facilitated Sessions: Joint Requirements Planning, Joint Application Design, User Group Meetings, Focus Groups	■ Intense, interactive sessions that include the end-users and the development team to define and refine requirements ■ Require skilled facilitator to maximize results ■ Effective if good relationships exist
Existing Materials	■ Review reports, documentation, codes tables, training materials ■ May not be current
Apprenticing, Observation, Videotaping Tasks, Work Flow and Process Walkthroughs	■ Provides opportunities to view actual work being done by end-users ■ Time commitment varies on approach used ■ Excellent source of details in data needs and processes ■ Can provide clues on unstated requirements
Package Reviews and Evaluations, Site Visits	■ Provides tangible applications to view ■ Can see what other functions may be desirable ■ Provides "expert" perspective and alternatives
Prototyping, Testing	■ Provides tangible view of the application ■ Later stages provide running portion of the application to be used ■ Good source of identifying exception handling
Application Support Help Desk, Bug Reports	■ Should be considered part of the application's end-user community ■ Excellent source of commonly-asked questions, problem areas, requested functionality
Sales and Marketing Teams, Market Research, Trade Shows, Internet & Electronic Forums	■ Provides additional perspectives on functions needed ■ Critical to use these techniques when developing for commercial market

viding. The interviewer basically asks questions and then clarifies the information provided. It is a good idea to bring two people to an interview—one to direct the interview and ask the questions, and the other to record the information. Listen to what is being said, as well as what is *not* being said. Be aware of political implications—"read between the lines."

The second technique is to "Think globally." This means to recognize what *all* the customers need and want. Since only a selection of the end-user community is providing input, remember that there are others who you are not seeing. With offices stretched across the country and around the world, many times "World Headquarters" provides all the input. Home office personnel do not always have a global view (as people in the other offices will tell you!). Ask questions about procedural differences, data differences, business event differences, hardware and software differences, language differences, paper sizes and report formatting needs, color usages, etc.

The third technique is to "Remain focused." It is very easy to be drawn into the existing system and its faults. End-users may only want to talk about its processes and needs, instead of the requirements of the new application. Use the information on the requirements from the existing system as a starting point for identifying the requirements of the new system.

Other techniques that should be used are described in Table 9-2. More information can be found on these techniques in various industry publications, trade journals, and industry professional associations.

SUMMARY

When defining and scoping an application, it is critical to not overlook the details. The details are uncovered by:

- Understanding the need for end-users
- Selecting the right people as end-users

- Effectively utilizing end-users
- Developing and maintaining open communication with end-users
- Successfully gathering requirements from end-users

Defining the details during the beginning of the project, by effectively involving end-users, and successfully gathering requirements will greatly increase a project's chances for success.

CHAPTER 10

AVOIDING ANALYSIS-PARALYSIS

Analyze:
To separate into parts or basic principles so as to determine
the nature of the whole; examine methodically

Paralyze:
To impair the progress or functioning of; make
inoperative or powerless

"Analysis-paralysis!" That phrase strikes fear into the hearts of many project managers and developers. Analysis-paralysis refers to the phenomenon of never moving out of the analysis effort and over-analyzing the requirements until the budget, resources, and need for the application are gone.

Many of the projects that fail do so because of analysis-paralysis. Open any trade journal and you'll find examples of these types of project failures. In those same journals, you'll find a myriad of "silver bullets"—the wonder-tools, the must-have training classes, and the consultants with the know-how (to say nothing of the excellent books that are available!).

While analysis is aided by good tools, consultants, and training, analysis fails when it is over done. Knowing when to stop analyzing and move on is a critical piece of knowledge. This knowledge comes, in part, from experience. Experience of the software developer and experience bundled in the development process, or methodology, being used by the project team. It is essential that the development process used provides guidance on knowing when to stop analysis.

Unfortunately, the traditional waterfall approach can contribute to analysis-paralysis. Since another sign-off was required at the end of the analysis phase, and this sign-off was treated as a solid scope document, there was significant risk in not doing thorough analysis. Project managers were afraid that if the requirements were not thoroughly analyzed, something substantial might be missed, resulting in project overruns, etc. So instead of finding a better way to gather requirements and negotiate scope, projects fell back on a faulty process and became too afraid to move forward. If you've seen a deer frozen in your headlights, you know the situation.

The development process discussed in earlier chapters avoids this pitfall. This development process utilizes overlap and iteration between stages. Ending analysis is not as "frightening" an event. When sign-off occurs, more information has been gathered and understood. The fear of missing requirements is minimized and scope can be more effectively negotiated.

Using an effective development approach, however, is only part of the solution for avoiding analysis-paralysis. For analysis to be effective:

- Agree on the purpose
- Know when to start
- Remain focused
- Use the appropriate techniques
- Remain implementation-independent
- Know when to stop

BEFORE BEGINNING ANALYSIS

Agree on the Purpose

When undertaking a task, clarify the goals or objectives of the task. This is especially true before starting any analysis tasks. If you ask the members of a typical project team what they think is accomplished during analysis, you will get the these responses:

- The end-user will tell you that a lot of complicated dia-grams are created that they don't really understand.
- The project manager will tell you that the scope changes daily during analysis.
- The developer will tell you that a lot of hair is pulled out and nights are spent dreaming of data flow diagrams.

Yes, all those things are accomplished, but what *should* be accomplished?

It is essential for the entire project team to agree on the goals and end-products of analysis. The methodology being used on the project will identify some general goals, but the project team must understand those goals and agree that they are the real goals. Once the project manager and developers are in agreement, the end-users must also agree. The first step in this process is to verify that the project team understands the term "analysis." Analysis is the act of breaking apart a list of requirements into its various smaller components. By understanding its components, a fuller understanding of the application as a whole is obtained. The physical result of analysis is a collection of models that illustrate the relationships between the various components of the application. To create these models, a process of information gathering, assessing, questioning, and discerning is completed. As illustrated in Figure 10–1, analysis aims to:

- Identify the relationships between the application components
- Build a solid understanding of the application requirements, including the business rules
- Verify and refine requirements

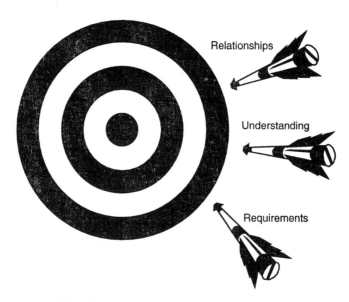

FIGURE 10–1.   The aims of analysis.

During analysis, you are building the full picture of the application's requirements. You are seeing the relationships between the various components, which the end-users described. You are identifying the data needs and relationships. For the purpose of ultimately building the best solution, you are understanding how the end-users complete their jobs and how the application is part of that process. You are learning about the various events that trigger different parts of that process. You are moving from a high, abstract level of understanding to a detailed, concrete level of understanding.

The second step in this agreement process is to agree that this detailed level of understanding is the focus; the focus is not to develop code and prototypes. Many times, analysis is rushed or ended prematurely because the end-users want to see "something other than models." There is a strong drive to move towards coding as soon as possible. It is critical to obtain agreement from all members of the analysis team that the focus is to develop understanding, not code.

The third step in this process is having the project team agree on the breadth of the analysis. To develop the full picture of the application, analysis must be completed with equal focus on all the application components:

- Data
- Events
- Processes
- Objects

Building the picture of the application requires seeing the view of all four components. This amount of analysis does not result in wasted time and effort; it results in a fuller picture and understanding of the application. For example, to fully appreciate the complexity and variety of the Grand Canyon, you must see it from the North Rim, the South Rim, and along the riverbed. Only after seeing it from those views, can you really grasp its magnificence.

The fourth, and final, step in building consensus is to agree on the scope of the analysis tasks. Verify with the analysis team the application that is being analyzed. Is it today's application or tomorrow's? Primarily, the requirements of tomorrow's system are being analyzed. However, if there is a current system, there are some benefits from briefly analyzing it.

Timebox the analysis of the existing system—you don't want to rebuild that system, but you do want to understand the relationships and rules between the data, events, and processes. Be aware, however, that what you are looking at is an implemented system—some relationships and rules will have been adjusted, mutated, and destroyed over time. Many processes will have been created to work around the old system that should not be repeated in the new system. Diagramming the relationships between data entities may provide some input on the finer points of business rules.

Know When to Start

Obtaining agreement on the purpose and goals of analysis is one factor that leads to effective analysis. Another critical factor is knowing the right time to start. Traditionally, analysis has been a distinct stage of a project. It started immediately after sign-off on requirements was obtained. During analysis, all the interview notes and survey results were reviewed and information was pulled out to start building the various models. Inevitably, some information had not been sufficiently gathered, which resulted in additional interviews and requirements changes. In this approach, the analysis effort was started too late into the project.

As Figure 10–2 illustrates, analysis should begin shortly after requirements-gathering has started. As soon as the first several interviews are completed, the analysis team has enough information to begin analyzing and modeling the requirements. During the first several requirements-gathering sessions, the key data entities will be uncovered. The relationships

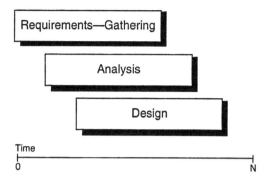

FIGURE 10-2. The development process: requirements-gathering, analysis, and design.

between them may not be clearly established, but that then provides the next set of questions to ask. The same is true for the business events and processes. In fact, questions about major business events, critical business processes, and essential data needs are good interview questions.

Analysis tasks are very similar to the requirements-gathering tasks: They are both focused on information—gathering and understanding it. There is great synergy in completing both sets of tasks in the same general timeframe:

■ The information gathered during requirements-gathering feeds directly into the analysis models.

■ Analysis can be conducted while the information is still "fresh" in the minds of the end-user and the analyst.

■ Analysis results can be clarified and verified during requirements-gathering sessions; iteration naturally occurs between requirements-gathering and analysis tasks.

■ Similar skills are needed to gather and then analyze requirements.

■ Many of the same end-users provide information on requirements and verify the analysis models.

■ Techniques, such as Joint Requirements Planning, can be used to both gather requirements and create initial analysis models.

■ Naming standards and conventions can be defined earlier, when the impact of change is less; these conventions also help clarify and verify the requirements and models as they encourage a common "language."

Recognition of these points of synergy helps the analysis team know when to start. The project manager should take this into account when developing the project schedule. Avoid the tendency (and habit) of starting analysis when requirements-gathering is between 75 percent and 100 percent complete. Start analysis when requirements-gathering is between 5 percent and 20 percent complete. As the intensity of requirements-gathering increases, so does that of analysis. But, as the requirements-gathering tasks are nearing 60 percent completion, the level of intensity drastically increases in analysis.

Unfortunately, these percentage ranges are wide; project scheduling is somewhat subjective, as every project has different variables. The key idea to remember is that there is synergy between the two types of tasks. If you start analysis at the right time, you will reap the benefits and avoid analysis-paralysis. You will have momentum on your side. You also will gather requirements more effectively and better understand them, thus avoiding the urge to over-analyze them before defining scope.

DURING ANALYSIS

Remain Focused

A cause of analysis-paralysis is straying from the purpose. That purpose was defined prior to starting analysis, but it is very easy to move into other areas and try to meet other goals. Remain focused on the purpose of analysis to develop a detailed, concrete understanding of the requirements. Analysis does not strive to re-engineer the business (that is dealt with to some extent during design). Analysis does not strive to develop prototypes; in fact, analysis should remain implementation-independent. Analysis focuses on "what" the application must do—what information must be provided, what processes must be supported, what business events must be acknowledged. Design and prototyping are concerned with the implementation of those requirements—how the application will deliver the information, how the application will perform processes, how the application will respond to specific events.

It is also important to remain focused on the application under study. It is very easy to be sidetracked into analyzing other applications, especially the existing system, when trying to understand the required relationships in the new system. For example, when implementing a new accounting system, it is very easy to document today's inefficient, legacy processes, instead of focusing on what the new system should do. Or analyze what happens in the billing system that feeds into the accounting system. Do not fall into that trap! Remember that it may be necessary to look into other applications, but *only* for the purpose of understanding the new one. Ask, "How is my application affected by what happens in this other application?" Do not try to understand the other application; focus only on the impact it has on your application.

Example—Investment Company

A company was replacing a financial reporting system. The system was to determine the current value of all the company's investments. The project team very quickly found out that the end-user team could only articulate their needs in terms of the existing system, which was a conglomeration of several long-standing applications. The analysis team, therefore, had to develop high-level models of the current system's data, events, and processes, before being able to assess what would be addressed in the new system.

It would have been very easy for the team to stray into a detailed analysis of the existing system:

- The end-users were comfortable talking about that system.
- The subject-matter was complex.
- The boundaries of the new system were very vague.

Instead, the team was disciplined and focused. They concentrated on understanding what the new system needed. They talked with the end-users in terms of "processes and data," and not "systems and components." Most importantly, they remained focused on their objective. They understood the existing systems to the extent necessary to identify the inputs and outputs of the new system. They were able to complete their analysis effectively and successfully determine the scope of the new system.

Use the Appropriate Techniques

Using the appropriate analysis techniques can also help avoid analysis-paralysis. During requirements-gathering, you pull from your "bag of tricks" the most appropriate techniques for gathering information. During analysis, you must select the best modeling techniques to now analyze that information.

There are a number of modeling techniques, each providing specific benefits. They also have their specific time and skills requirements. You must review the project and its selected methodology and determine which modeling techniques will deliver the best results. Table 10–1 describes the most popular modeling techniques.

Historically, data and process modeling have been used the most. Over the last several years, event modeling has moved into the mainstream. Currently, object-oriented analysis

TABLE 10-1.   MODELING TECHNIQUES

Technique	Definition	Major Deliverables
Data	Understand and model the application's data requirements, including attributes and relationships.	■ Entity-Relationship Diagram ■ Entity Definitions ■ Attribute Definitions ■ Relationship/Business Rule Definitions
Process	Understand and model the internal processing behavior of the application.	■ Context Diagram ■ Data Flow Diagrams ■ Work Flow Diagrams ■ Function Decomposition Diagrams
Event	Understand and model the application's response to business transactions and events.	■ Event List ■ Event Descriptions ■ Event/Stimulus/Response Matrix ■ State Transition Diagrams
Object	Understand and model the application's objects and their interactions.	■ Class Model ■ Use Case Descriptions ■ Object Interaction Diagram

is being embraced by the IT industry and is gaining popularity. The object-oriented analysis methods are still encountering some consolidation of terminology and philosophy that will eventually result in a more cohesive and clear approach. The other modeling approaches have been used for many years and a stable process and toolset currently exists for each.

Using one and only one technique is not sufficient. You need a combination of techniques to get the "Grand Canyon" big picture. At the very least, you must model data, events, and processes. Modeling only the data of the application is not sufficient—what is done to the data and when? Modeling only the processes is not sufficient—what triggers the process and what is needed? Modeling only the events is not sufficient—what happens after the event and how? And unless you are using a full object-oriented implementation approach, including the use of an object-oriented database, object-oriented analysis is not sufficient.

The bottom line is to use whatever techniques are necessary to develop that detailed understanding of the application's requirements and their relationships. The techniques you will use depend on:

- The models that end-users are accustomed to using and reviewing;
- The development team's familiarity with the application's functionality;
- The end-users' familiarity with the application's functionality;
- The level of sophistication and experience with each approach;
- The size and complexity of the application;
- The available time for learning new approaches;
- The development approach and methodology; and
- The culture of the IT organization.

The modeling technique you use first depends on your project and your own personal style. It also depends, in part, on the information you receive first. In a sense, analysis is like building a puzzle—everyone has their own approach. Some people start with the frame, others find the corner pieces first, others find a theme and build around it, others put it together by picking up random pieces and setting them in place. Regardless of they way you build a puzzle, you must not lose any pieces and you must find the right place for each piece. You may even have some pieces left over that don't belong.

Remain Implementation-Independent

Another cause of analysis-paralysis is focusing on the implementation of the requirements. Analysis is a time of open thinking and of pursuing ideas. It is the time to focus on "what" the application must do, not "how." You must not be thinking about what the windows and reports would look like to support the process or how performance would be impacted by certain data relationships.

Allowing implementation considerations to influence the analysis results is dangerous. For example, when analyzing the data requirements, it is easy to think in terms of tables and rows. Decisions can then be made, consciously or unconsciously, that compromise the true data relationships and business rules. Design is the time that these decisions are made; analysis is when the base is created to make those decisions.

It is not easy to remain implementation-independent. The analyst must be a big picture thinker and not get mired in the details. There is a fine line, though, because the analyst needs to understand the details and their impact on other components of the application. You must train yourself to take a mental "step-back" every now and then and look at the models. Ask yourself, "What's missing? What doesn't make sense? Where is there overlap? Where are things compromised?"

Remember during this process that the end-users are not experts with your modeling techniques. They shouldn't be, either! They don't speak in terms of data flows, triggers, and object interaction. You must listen to what they are saying and determine what they are not saying. Be careful—many times, the end-users are defining their business processes from a data perspective. They are used to using data-driven mainframe applications, where the processes were determined solely by data availability. Some of the end-users you speak with have no other way of knowing what the process is, or should be.

You will identify gaps in their processes and data due to problems in the existing applications. Do not model these implementation constraints—remember you want to focus on the new application and not re-create the existing one. It is sometimes difficult to distinguish between the two.

CONCLUDING ANALYSIS

Just as it is important to know when to start analysis, it is important to know when to stop. Projects have failed because they just kept analyzing and analyzing and . . . . Analysis tasks do not have concrete objectives that are easy to measure. You don't have a quota on business objects or data flows. It is hard to quantify if people have an understanding of the application or not.

Remember that analysis is being done in conjunction with design. When analysis overlaps and iterates with design, it is easier to determine when to stop than when using a traditional waterfall process. Use the process to your advantage.

Also, timebox the analysis tasks. Put a limit on the time allocated to analysis. At the end of that time period, assess your results. If the results are not favorable, schedule another period of analysis. At the end of that period, assess. It may be time to stop analysis when:

- No new data entities, events, or objects are identified;
- Modifications to models are minor; and/or
- Terminology and naming is not changing.

When allocating time to analysis tasks, do not scrimp. It is tempting to limit the time spent in analysis, in order to begin producing prototypes and "code." Avoid the pressure, since you will only make up the time (and more) during design, construction, and testing.

SUMMARY

Analysis is the act of breaking apart a list of requirements into its various smaller components to develop a fuller understanding of the application. Analysis quite often fails because the project team and end-users cannot agree that they are ready to move on. Analysis will be effective if you:

- Agree on the purpose
- Know when to start
- Remain focused
- Use the appropriate techniques
- Remain implementation-independent
- Know when to stop

CHAPTER **11**

DESIGNING FOR SUCCESS

Design:
To plan out in systematic, usually graphic form

Success:
The achievement of something desired, planned, or attempted

157

Design is an exciting stage of the development process. It is exciting to create concrete views of the application and see how the abstract models and lists of requirements will be fulfilled. It is fun to see a window mock-up that shows real customer information. It is rewarding to detail the flow between dialogs and how they are to be built in the various modules. While requirements-gathering is a listening task and analysis is a thinking task, design is a creative task. Design, however, is not creativity just for the sake of creativity. The project team cannot design without process, objectives, or techniques. That would result in project failure.

For design to be successful, the project team must:

- Follow the right design process
- Focus on the end-users' processes
- Utilize prototyping effectively and efficiently
- Employ appropriate design techniques

Design must not be confused with prototyping. Prototyping is a technique that is used during the design process and results in the development of better designs. Prototyping is the technique of putting the design into a form that is closer to its final, physical implementation. This allows for better review and understanding. [Note: Prototyping is explained in more detail later in this chapter.]

THE DESIGN PROCESS

Since design is a creative task, it is essential that the team follow a clearly defined process. This process provides a structure that moves the design effort forward. The design process followed by the project team must:

- Meet the proper objectives
- Occur at the right point in time

■ Create the necessary deliverables
■ Incorporate architecture decisions
■ Control scope effectively
■ Involve end-users appropriately

Objectives

The primary objective of the design stage is to create specifications of the application sufficient for construction to begin. The amount of time spent in design depends on the complexity and size of the application, as well as the experience level of the construction team. A more experienced team requires less detailed specifications.

Traditionally, design has focused only on meeting this objective. More and more, however, design is successfully fulfilling other objectives in the development process. Design, coupled with prototyping tools and techniques, is being used to aid in the requirements discovery process, as well as to illustrate analysis results. Design very quickly tells you if the processes make sense as you have documented them. Design also very quickly identifies business rules that were not properly understood.

For design to be successful, the project team must understand these various design objectives. They must clearly understand how design is being used on their project, and be committed to meeting the stated objectives. The process that is used must support these objectives by incorporating the right tasks and techniques at the right time, which creates the right deliverables.

Timing

These objectives are best met when design is done in conjunction with requirements gathering and analysis. As discussed in *Chapter 9: Defining the Details* and *Chapter 10: Avoiding Analysis-*

Paralysis, there is much synergy between these three stages. Each stage benefits from the knowledge simultaneously gained in the other two stages. Figure 11–1 demonstrates the timing of the design stage relative to the other stages.

As Figure 11–1 illustrates, not much time needs to elapse between the start of requirements-gathering and design. You are ready to begin the design process almost immediately after requirements-gathering and analysis have started. Remember, though, that in the beginning, there will be many rapid changes as information is gathered and understood. So, if you start design very early in the process, be prepared to revise over and over.

Deliverables

In fact, during the early part of design, the time is best spent developing templates that will be used throughout the entire design process. For example, as you identify the major business processes and end-user tasks, design the overall Dialog Navigation Model. The Dialog Navigation Model is the template for the entire user interface. It is essentially the main menu bar with the corresponding menu options. This model is the outline of the major end-user tasks and business processes.

Create templates, or design outlines, of the window types that will be needed based on those identified processes. Create

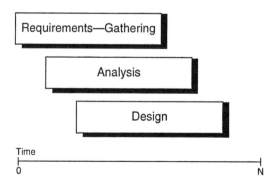

FIGURE 11–1. The development process: requirements-gathering, analysis, and design.

templates of the different types of reports needed as system outputs. Identify key database tables and columns. Identify the critical modules and the relationships between them.

As design progresses, the details of the application are then filled in. The design outlines are created initially, they are presented to the end-users for review, new requirements are identified, the outlines are modified, and the cycle continues. Eventually, the full set of design deliverables is created and fleshed out. The design is then complete for the user interface (windows, documentation, help), database, business logic, reports and interfaces, and architecture.

Incorporating Architecture Decisions

During analysis, the details of the implementation are ignored. The team is focusing on "what" the application will do, not "how" it will be done. During design, the focus shifts to implementation. The "how's" become important. In fact, implementation considerations become the constraints on the design. For example, the ideal window design for a given end-user task may require four different windows, each with a small amount of data and processing. When implemented, this design could have significant productivity problems. The designer must assess the design and determine if it is the best possible implementation of the functionality. Could a more efficient method of completing the task be designed, even if it breaks some GUI design principles? The application priorities identified during requirements-gathering should drive the decisions. If performance is more important than usability, then the design principles will be sacrificed in order to meet the productivity requirements.

Database designs are also significantly impacted by implementation considerations. Any good database architect will tell you that the logical database design is normalized to fourth or fifth normal form, but the physical database is de-normalized in order to save on disk space, read/write accesses, and data redundancy. This is the way it must be!

Architecture decisions also become important during design. The decisions made regarding features of the architecture are also design constraints. For example, the window management system being used will limit some of the features that can be designed into the user interface. The structure of the architecture may also limit how much data can be sent from the client to the server at any one time. This impacts the window design and messaging.

The architecture team must be involved in the review cycle of the designs. They are in the best position to determine if what was designed is feasible, given the architecture designed. The Functional Architect and the Technical Architect must work closely together to identify critical modifications to the designs of the architecture. They also communicate the changes to their teams for implementation.

Scope Control

As Figure 11–2 shows, the design process is an iterative process. Remember, too, that this process is occurring within the larger iterative cycle illustrated in Figure 11–1. It is very

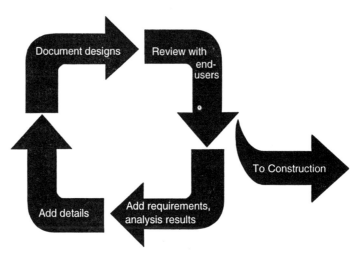

FIGURE 11–2.   The design process.

easy to continue design and gradually increase scope. The project manager must establish clear parameters on the duration of design and at what point the scope is defined. At that point, the project manager, the key end-users, and the end-user management must agree that the project scope has been sufficiently defined. This agreement will help limit (but not eliminate) future scope creep.

One way to define the scope is to divide the application into functional groups. Functional groups are the major pieces of functionality provided by the application. A functional group consists of a set of windows, reports, and back-end processes that, when combined, provide a business function that has value to the end-users.

Functional groups are identified by analyzing the Context Diagram, corresponding Data Flow Diagrams, and Event Descriptions. Look for the major business processes and business events on those models. Using the End-User Profiles, identify common functions used by each group of end-users. Also, there is a high correlation between functional groups and major menu items documented on the Dialog Navigation Model.

Once the groups are identified, estimates can be created for the coding and testing portions of the development process, including the corresponding architecture components. Dependencies between functional groups, the application's priorities, and the implementation estimates are all used by the project manager to identify the components of the application that are within scope of the project. It is this list of functional groups that the end-user management must then agree are the scope of the current project. Refer to *Chapter 8: Knowing the End-Result* for more information on scoping projects.

End-User Involvement

Design will not be completely successful if the end-users are not involved. It is essential that they are involved early and often in the design process. End-users cannot be involved only for design reviews and usability tests. They must be involved in task analysis, process re-engineering, and prototyping sessions. Make sure that the end-users involved during the design stage have a good understanding of the entire business process, as well as an understanding of the detailed steps. It may be necessary to have different end-users for each of the identified functional groups. Refer to *Chapter 9: Defining the Details* for a thorough discussion of involving the right end-users on the project.

DESIGNING FOR END-USER PROCESSES

What Drives Design?

An application consists of many components:

- User interface
- Business processes and functionality
- Database
- Underlying architecture

These components must all be designed somewhat concurrently. [Note: Database and architecture design is addressed in *Chapter 13: Creating the Architecture.*] Project managers tend to structure the project team into smaller teams, based on the portion of the application they will design. There is a sub-team of database architects/designers, a sub-team of graphical user interface (GUI) designers, etc. This division is not a bad thing because each area requires a distinct set of skills and deliverables.

A negative side-effect of this division, however, is the loss of focus on the big picture. There also tends to be a bit of arguing as to which sub-team drives the design process. Traditionally, the database sub-team drove the design of the user interface (UI) and business logic. In a mainframe data-centric application, everything was dependent on the availability of data. In a way, the data driving the design of the UI made sense.

Today, however, the data cannot drive the design process. If it does, the application will not be as usable and efficient as it could be. The result will be traditional screens with a little GUI flare. You've seen those—they're not pretty. GUI screens are not "pure data-entry" screens. They reflect the end-user's processes. Good GUI screens are used to query, enter, and modify data. They illustrate business rules and logic. If GUI screens were intended to be data-centric, there would be no need for pop-up windows or list boxes that offered choices in a user-driven order!

To be effective, design must be driven by the business needs of the application. Design must answer the question "What will best serve the end-user?" All design issues are influenced more by the business processes and the end-users' tasks than by any other concern. Design is driven by the concern for the overall picture—data, events, and processes—not what is easiest for the architecture to provide. Nor what makes for the easiest GUI to build, nor what makes for the most efficient database structure.

If the business needs drive the design process, then the application will provide the functionality to the end-user in the most effective, usable manner.

User Interface

A key component of the application is the user interface. To the end-user, the user interface *is* the application. Most people think the UI is just the screens/windows that the end-user uses to interact with the system. In reality, the UI consists of those screens, plus help, documentation, and training. These four components must be viewed as one and be consistent. All pieces must be of high quality. Remember that the end-users' perception of the application will be based on the screens, help, documentation, and training. In many cases, the end-user's perception has caused applications to be rejected because of spelling mistakes. "If there are simple mistakes in the help, imagine what mistakes there are behind the scenes!"

Specific skillsets are required to build each component of the user interface [Note: Refer to *Chapter 4: Building the Best Team* for a detailed discussion of skill requirements]. A common approach for organizing teams during the design and construction stages is to base the teams on the application components being built. Therefore, the programmers only see the screens and associated help (and error) messages. The training, documentation, and detailed help are developed by another team of people who interact with the rest of the development team on a limited basis. Unfortunately, this team division only encourages the perception among the "technical" personnel that the user interface only consists of the screens. This team division, when done poorly, also contributes to an inconsistent user interface.

All components of the user interface should be treated with equal importance. Help, documentation, and training should be designed as the screens are designed, not at the end of the testing stage. The overall structure and level of support must be determined during the design stage. Documentation, training, and help should be prototyped to demonstrate to the end-users what level of support will be available. The people building all four components should act as members of the same team. There needs to be very strong communication between the people designing the screens and the people developing the help, documentation, and training.

Training Design Tips. The team of people designing the training materials must follow an appropriate process. The training development process includes the following high-level steps:

1. Identify the groups of people requiring training on the new application.

2. Categorize the groups into audiences (business end-user, management, operations and support, maintenance, help desk, etc.).

3. Define each audience category.

4. Determine the training objectives for each audience category.

5. Identify the concepts that must be taught to meet the objectives.

6. Group the concepts into training modules.

7. Select the training delivery approach (instructor-led, computer-based training, self-study, on-the-job, etc.) most appropriate for each module.

8. Create an outline (curriculum plan) of each training module listing the audience, topics, time, prerequisites, materials requirements, and technical requirements; review and refine the outline.

9. Identify case studies needed for training activities; document objectives and appropriate scenarios.

10. Create and prototype standards for training materials; review and refine.

During the construction stage of the development process, the designs will be used to build the final training materials. These materials will then be tested and rolled-out. This process is discussed in more detail in *Chapter 12: Putting It All Together*.

Other important considerations for designing training materials include:

■ Assign quality resources to the training design tasks. Do not expect programmers to know how to design (or build) professional, value-added training materials. Just as you would not expect training developers to write code, do not expect programmers to write training materials.

■ Do not underestimate the training design or development effort. Start the design of training materials at the same time as the design of the rest of the user interface. The time and effort required to develop quality training materials can be as much as 20 percent of the total project effort. Projects can fail when the training effort is underestimated.

■ Prepare the end-user organization to maintain the training materials. Involve the end-users responsible for the ongoing delivery and maintenance in the design effort. Value their input as much as the input from the other end-users involved in the project.

Documentation and Help Design Tips. Documentation design is very similar to training design. The process and considerations are similar. The audience categories are also similar:

■ Business end-users and management

■ Operations personnel

■ Support and help desk personnel

■ Maintenance personnel

The content of the documentation, just like the training content, is tailored to the needs of each group of users, or audience. There will be various levels of documentation that are produced for each audience. For example, management may only use a limited number of application functions on an infrequent basis. They would need a "roadmap" of the functions they use in a very user-friendly format. Other business users may need overview documentation, which highlights the major functions that would be used during a start-up period. They would also need documentation that walks them through each function, as well as reference documentation that delves into the details of each screen and report.

Just like training, there are multiple ways of delivering documentation content to the end-users. During the design stage, the team must determine how each documentation module will be delivered. Documentation is really just a mechanism for delivering information and assistance to the end-user. Documentation can be delivered via hard-copy manuals, CD-ROM's of on-line reference materials, on-line help embedded within the application, or a combination. Traditionally, this information and assistance was provided in a very passive format: hard-copy manuals. The development team could never feel comfortable that the information would be readily available to the end-user.

■ Where would manuals be located?

■ Would they be updated?

■ Would anyone use them?

■ Why bother?

Today, with the GUI technology that is available, help systems can provide better and more effective assistance to the end-user. With most client/server applications, some level of hard-copy documentation for the business end-users is replaced by an on-line help system. An on-line help system can consist of:

■ Wizards and help agents that provide guidance in completing tasks;

■ Error, warning, and informational messages, presented through dialog boxes;

■ Simple definitions or instructions, displayed on the screen's message bar; and

■ Field-level help, screen-level help, and function-level help, accessed via the help menu item.

During design, decisions must be made as to the complexity of the help system.

■ What levels of help will be supported?

■ Will the development tools being used support that decision?

■ What are the priorities of the application—how much support is desired?

■ What documentation will be presented through on-line help versus through hard-copy manuals?

■ What are the limitations of the selected help development tools and how does that impact the level of support that can be provided?

During design, other decisions regarding documentation and help must be made:

■ If a packaged application is being used, will we supplement the vendor documentation or replace it? How can we modify the help, or incorporate our own help files?

■ Will the content in the hard-copy manual be the same as the on-line help content? What documentation and help tools can be used to maximize the synergy between the two efforts?

■ Will the application be translated into other languages? What is the impact on the documentation and the help? Who is responsible for translation? What standards must be modified to ensure that the same levels of help can be provided to all end-users?

■ How will the documentation and help be maintained during development? How often will changes be made and reviewed? What version control tools will be used? What are their limitations?

■ How will the help content be created? Will error, warning, informational, and message bar help be written in an external file, referenced by the code? Or will it be embedded in the code? What approach will the development tools support? How will the technical writers access the code to create, test, and refine the text? Will the programmers do those tasks? What is the impact on performance using this approach?

Screen Design Tips. Design of the GUI, or screens, is a complex task. Many times, designers start with one screen, move on to another, and another, etc. The result is an unstructured collection of screens. Re-use and maintainability are concepts that are laughable. A more effective approach to designing the screens is described in Table 11–1.

GUI design is an iterative process. The trick to keeping GUI design "under control" is to keep it simple. Use screen templates whenever possible. Adhere to GUI design standards—spend the time and money to buy or develop a comprehensive set. Divide the application into functional groups and assign teams based on those groups. Work on the most critical functional groups first. Within those groups, focus on the standard processing first. Don't be distracted by the exceptions to the standard. Keep a list of all possible exceptions and "what if" situations. Then, address exception processing once the standard, vanilla situations are stable and agreed upon. Figure 11–3 shows one way of managing the design process iterations.

Business Process Design

For an application to be effective, the GUI design cannot be separated from the business processes. The flow between various screens and the tasks accomplished by the end-users is just another view of the business processes. The business process design fills in the "missing pieces," or "black box" operations, from the end-users' perspective.

Design of the business processes (also known as application logic or business logic) addresses the functionality that the application provides. Specifically, this piece of design addresses what happens outside the end-users' view. It answers the following questions:

■ When does data need to be provided or accessed? How?

■ What processes need to take place when leaving screen A and going to screen B? What should happen to that data?

TABLE 11–1.   GUI DESIGN APPROACH

Task	Description	Major Deliverables
1. Identify overall main functions	Using Work Flow Diagrams and the Object Diagram, identify the major objects of the application and their associated major processes.	■ Menu Bar Items ■ Menu Bar Item Descriptions ■ Dialog Navigation Model
2. Associate functional groups with main functions	Review the menu bar items and determine the functional group to which each belongs; describe each functional group.	■ Functional Group Descriptions
3. Conduct task analysis	For each functional group, analyze the tasks the end-user completes for each business process. Determine which steps can be automated and which will remain manual. Focus on the standard tasks first and when they are stable, analyze exception processing.	■ Task Flow Diagrams ■ Standard Tasks Descriptions ■ Exception Handling Descriptions
4. Identify screens and dialog flow	Based on the task analysis, identify the screens. Determine the flow between screens needed to complete a task (dialog). Describe the purpose of each screen, critical processing, and key data. Begin with standard processing and primary screens.	■ List of Screens ■ Screen Descriptions ■ Dialog Flow Diagram

TABLE 11–1.   GUI DESIGN APPROACH (continued)

Task	Description	Major Deliverables
5. Design screens	Complete a layout of each screen, following GUI design standards. Correlate each field to the correct database field. Complete a Control-Action-Response Diagram to document the detailed processing for each screen. Use proto-typing and Joint Application Design techniques when appropriate.	■ Screen Design ■ Control-Action-Response Diagram
6. Review, refine, repeat	Have all screen designs audited against GUI design standards and screen templates. Complete usability testing on critical screens (requires that screens be "mocked up" in appropriate tool or language). Complete design reviews with end-user for primary screens. Incorporate only approved changes.	■ Audit Results ■ Usability Test Plans ■ Usability Test Results ■ Design Review Feedback ■ List of Approved Changes ■ List of Future Changes

■ What information should be presented on reports? When and how are those reports produced?

The Data Flow Diagrams and Function Decomposition Diagrams provide the basis for answering these questions. These answers are then refined during the task analysis process. These diagrams provide the break-down of the steps in each

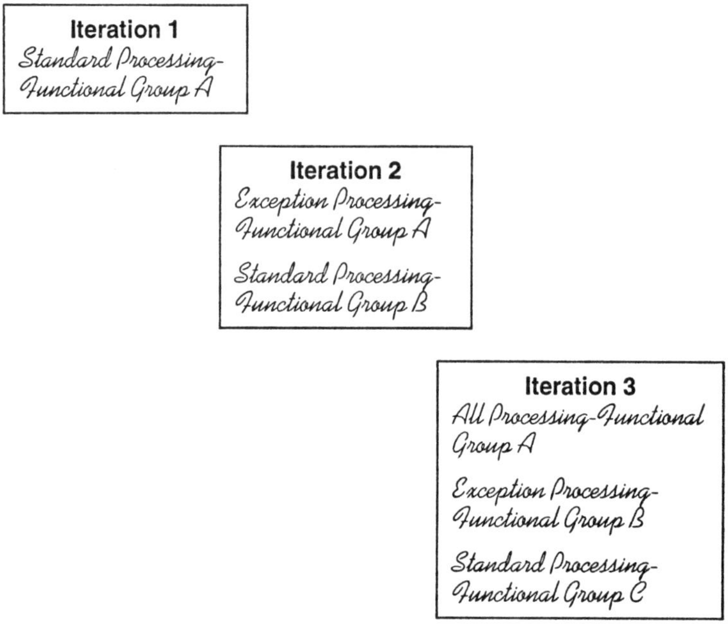

Iteration 1
Standard Processing-
Functional Group A

Iteration 2
Exception Processing-
Functional Group A

Standard Processing-
Functional Group B

Iteration 3
All Processing-Functional
Group A

Exception Processing-
Functional Group B

Standard Processing-
Functional Group C

FIGURE 11-3.   Design iterations.

process from an internal or system view. The designer's job is to then determine which processes are met by screens and which are met by non-UI modules. The designer must also determine which logic will be on the client, on the server, or met by triggers in the database. The designer also follows the reusability strategy to identify reusable modules, within and across applications.

During this portion of design, a need for re-engineering may be encountered. As the end-users are describing their tasks, you may identify inefficiencies and redundancies. The extent of re-engineering allowed in your project will be determined by schedule, availability, and politics. Small process changes may be permitted within the scope of the project and associated training. Major changes, such as job changes, work flow modifications, and new processes, will need to be assessed in cost/benefit terms. As a designer, never modify the end-users' task flow without their permission and that of the project manager.

There needs to be strong communication between the people doing the GUI design (front-end) and the people designing the business logic (back-end). Ideally, they are part of the same design team, based on functional groups. It is very important that the GUI designer and the functional designer understand what portion of the processing is done by the screen module and what is done by a called module. Both designers need to agree on what is best for performance, reusability, and maintainability. Compromises will need to be made by both designers. Assumptions can be made by neither. Both designers must also work with the database designers and technical architect to assess the feasibility and impact of their designs.

EFFECTIVE PROTOTYPING

According to the American Heritage Dictionary, a prototype is "an original type, form, or instance that serves as a model on which later stages are based." Over the last several years, prototyping has been considered a "silver bullet" and has become part of almost every developer's jargon. The availability of relatively affordable and easy prototyping tools has encouraged the use of prototyping. In some cases, prototyping has been misused. It has been used as a "complete" development process, as a replacement for requirements-gathering and analysis, and as a substitute for solid design.

Prototyping is an effective tool for testing and solidifying designs. It is also a very effective tool to help with the discovery of requirements. Prototyping critical screens and the flow between them makes the functionality "real" to the end-users. They can then tell you what pieces of information they forgot to mention, or took for granted. Also, prototyping the standard processing helps to identify the exception processing that must be supported.

Types of Prototyping

To utilize prototyping efficiently and effectively, the entire application should not be prototyped. Prototyping takes resources and time and, therefore, has a cost. To be effective, you should only prototype the areas that are risky and will benefit from prototyping. The following items are general items to be prototyped:

■ Overall application look-and-feel, including the on-line help system

■ Menu bar items and overall application navigation

■ Standard processing in critical functional groups

■ Functionality that is defined differently by various end-users

■ Frequently used screens

■ Complex or new functionality

■ Technically complex or risky areas

Each of these items will not be prototyped to the same level of detail. Some items do not require a detailed, fully functioning, highly interactive prototype. You are simply looking for agreement on concepts and general approaches. Table 11–2 describes the two primary types of prototypes and their objectives.

Low-fidelity prototyping is the appropriate technique for prototyping concepts and general approaches. Low-fidelity prototyping is less involved and requires less of an investment to obtain benefits. It is most effective in the early iterations of the design process, when higher-level issues are being resolved.

High-fidelity prototyping is more involved. A high-fidelity prototype is more robust and deeper in its capabilities. This kind of prototype is highly interactive and may even allow the end-users to enter non-specified data. High-fidelity

TABLE 11–2.   TYPES OF PROTOTYPING

Name	Description	Objectives
Low-Fidelity	■ Limited functionality and interaction ability ■ Many times are paper-based "mock-ups" ■ If coding is done, it will not be reused; is "quick and dirty" ■ Can be completed by the Interface Designer	■ Demonstrate general look and feel ■ Demonstrate overall application navigation ■ Provide proof-of-concept to the end-users and implementation team ■ Obtain consensus on design templates ■ Decide between multiple design options ■ Refine and discover requirements and exception processing
High-Fidelity	■ Fully interactive and deep functionality for given area ■ More refined require preparation of realistic data ■ In later stages, code should be well-structured and evolve into final application ■ Requires Interface Programmer to complete	■ Provide semi-realistic example of anticipated performance ■ Assess the technical feasibility of several design options

prototypes are used in the later iterations of the design process when trying to finalize specifics.

OTHER DESIGN TECHNIQUES

Joint Application Design

No discussion of design would be complete without mentioning Joint Application Design (JAD). JAD is an effective design technique in which the design team and the end-user team come together and jointly design critical portions of the application. A facilitator, or meeting leader, is used to keep the session on track. There are many good reference books available on JAD techniques and the formal process.

It is easy to abuse JAD in the same ways as prototyping. JAD, when combined with prototype review sessions, can be an effective way of finalizing requirements, exception processing, and design issues. Teams that have been meeting and working with their end-users in a "healthy" way have said that they have been using JAD techniques forever! Sometimes, JAD is formally used when the IT organization and end-user organization have not worked together successfully before, or when there are intense politics operating in the project team.

Design Documentation

It is essential that design decisions are documented. With the easy-to-use design and code generation tools available, there is a strong temptation to not "put anything on paper." Don't give in! The time that is "saved" during design by not documenting will be more than used during coding, testing, and maintenance. Develop some simple documentation templates for the task analysis results, screen descriptions, and module designs. The Control-Action-Response Diagram is a simple, yet powerful, document for all users of the screen design. Yes, there is an overhead cost in developing documentation, but the downstream savings is its benefit. Don't create detailed documentation during the early iterations of the designs. During the early iterations, create descriptions that specify the purpose of the screen or module and the primary processing that must occur. Create the detailed documentation of the layouts and logic in the later iterations, when fewer big changes will be required. The project manager must create the process by which the documentation is created and verified. If you are using outside designers and programmers, this documentation is even more critical.

SUMMARY

Design is the process of detailing, in a systematic manner, the specifics of the application. It is the process of determining how functionality will be delivered in the application. Design is the creative stage of the development process, but must have parameters to be effective. For design to be successful, the project team must:

- Follow the right design process
- Focus on the end-users' processes
- Utilize prototyping effectively and efficiently
- Employ appropriate design techniques

CHAPTER 12

PUTTING IT ALL TOGETHER

Construct:
To form by assembling or combining parts; build

Test:
A procedure for critical evaluation; a means of determining the presence, quality, or truth of something; a trial

Implement:
To put into practical effect; carry out

Putting it all together—what a rewarding thought! Of course, that phrase implies that you have all the parts you need. Requirements-gathering, analysis, and design have focused on identifying and gathering all those parts. Now, construction, testing, and implementation will deliver those parts into a cohesive, functioning whole.

Just because a project team has gotten to this point does not mean that they have automatically achieved success. Here, many client/server projects fail. The construction, testing, and implementation stages of the development cycle are just as critical as the earlier stages.

There are two major factors that contribute to project success at this juncture:

■ Beginning at the most effective and efficient time
■ Employing the appropriate techniques for each stage

As discussed in previous chapters, client/server development success requires an iterative, overlapping process. Traditionally, construction did not start until all design work was completed and signed-off. Testing did not start until major portions of the application were coded. With client/server development, construction and testing must begin sooner. As Figure 12–1 illustrates, construction and testing are well underway by the time the design stage is completed. Beginning these stages at the proper time will enhance the project's chances for success.

The other major success factor relates to employing the proper techniques and tools for construction, testing, and implementation. There are solid, proven techniques for each stage of the development process. These techniques should be used to increase project success. The rest of this chapter looks in detail at the success factors for the construction, testing, and implementation stages.

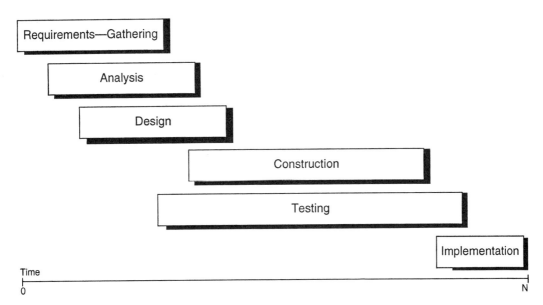

FIGURE 12–1.   The development process.

CONSTRUCTION

Construction, in the software development process, is the process of creating tangible, concrete representations of the application. Construction involves the tasks related to programming and unit (or preliminary) testing. Programming refers to the building of executable pieces of the application. Programming may be done with the help of a multitude of development tools, 4th-generation-languages (4GL), or object-oriented languages. Or it may be done in a programming language such as C or COBOL.

To be successful, construction must:

■ Begin at the appropriate time
■ Utilize tools, re-use, and standards
■ Consider unit testing part of the scope

Timing

Figure 12–1 shows where construction starts in an overlapped development process. Construction begins early in this process; it does not wait for the completion of design. This approach makes sense when you remember that the application is being designed functional group by functional group. As defined in *Chapter 11: Designing for Success,* functional groups are the major pieces of functionality provided by the application, consisting of a set of windows, reports, and back-end processes that combined provide a business function that has value to the end-user. The entire set of functional groups is prioritized by benefit, importance, complexity, and criticality.

As design and prototyping for the most critical groups is completed, they can then be built and tested. The prototypes are used as detailed designs from which the final versions are built. A common mistake is to build and test the small, simple components of the application first, leaving the critical and difficult pieces to the end, when time is precious and the chance of failure is greater.

Development of the prototypes is not considered part of construction, even though similar technical skills are needed for both stages. Prototypes provided design input to help us arrive at this point. Construction should remain focused on the development of the final deliverable application. Construction also includes the tasks involved in repairing problems in programs discovered during the testing stage.

Tools, Re-use, and Standards

Just as other stages of the development process benefit from the use of tools, construction can benefit from the use of programming, version control, and documentation tools. Today, portions of the client/server construction process have been automated. It is foolish to disregard the benefits these tools can provide, such as productivity improvements, tighter cleaner code, and reusability.

As discussed in *Chapter 6: Establishing the Development Infrastructure*, the development environment must include team version control tools, Graphical User Interface (GUI) testing tools, and a variety of standards. The products used must also be able to support larger team efforts. Many tools are suitable for small teams of two to six developers, but are not robust or stable enough for larger teams. Many cannot support cross-team development efforts, either. The project manager must verify that the tools selected as part of the development environment will meet the specific needs of the project.

A benefit of using the appropriate development tools is the creation of reusable components. Creation and use of reusable components is also a technique that enhances the success of construction. Reusability refers to the multiple use of components within one application, or from one application to another. Components can be stored in a class library or an object repository. They can be developed in any of a number of different object-oriented or object-based languages, created using structured programming techniques, or purchased from component vendors. Regardless of how components are implemented, they must be error free, fully functional, well documented, version controlled, and accessible by the entire construction team. Objects that must be recreated by other team members or future development efforts will not provide the long-term leverage intended.

Use of development tools and reusable components will not guarantee construction success. Chaos will still reign if standards are not followed. Just as the overall development process requires standardization, so does the construction stage. Also, reusable components cannot be created without the construction team following various standards. These standards are part of the development environment. Standards required for construction include:

■ Coding
■ Naming
■ Data structures and files

■ Unit testing
■ Development tool usage guidelines
■ Reusability guidelines

Unit Testing

Unit testing, sometimes called preliminary testing, is the initial testing of the code. The person who wrote the code is responsible for conducting some overall testing on it. Unit testing verifies that the program:

■ Technically performs as it should;
■ Collects the proper input and produces the proper output, as determined by field specifications; and
■ Branches to the appropriate logic at the appropriate time.

Successful unit testing requires clear design documents, especially good descriptions of business logic and calculations. Many organizations feel that the programmer should not, and cannot, perform unit testing. Nonsense! If programmers are not responsible for completing unit testing, then they have no incentive to produce clean solid code. They rely on the testing team to verify their work. The testing team becomes code "proofreaders" and the programmers are simply typists and not writers. Programmers benefit greatly from unit testing—they gain a better understanding of the program's functions and can verify that they have built the most efficient, maintainable, flexible code based on that understanding.

Programmers who have fully unit-tested their code are willing to expose their work to the testing team and the end-user community. Because of the iterative nature of client/server development, this exposure is needed sooner than in the traditional development process. Client/server development proceeds faster when the programmers are confident in the cleanliness of their work. They are able to ensure that there is sufficient progress for each iteration of testing and feedback. If there is not adequate progress, the end-user will not actively focus on the evolving solution. Also, if there are noticeable errors, the end-user will lose confidence in the project and the application's quality.

TESTING

Testing is the art of verification. Testing answers the question, "Does the application produce the expected, desired result, time after time?" The key to successful testing is clearly knowing, to a detailed level, what the application should and shouldn't do.

Testing is also the art of knowing when to stop. There is a fine line between completing testing efficiently and lowering your quality standards. Testing requires a real perspective—knowing what is acceptable for today. Testing cannot end before the critical problems are fixed, but how do you define critical? The definitions of "critical," "problem," "enhancement," and "fixed" must be determined and agreed upon prior to starting testing. In the heat of the testing kitchen, you will not be able to define parameters in a sensible manner.

When testing, push the application to its limits. Make the application "blow up and crash." See what it takes to reach that point.

- Is it acceptable?
- Does the application come to a standstill when 15 users hit "Enter" at the same time?
- Or does it take more than 50 users?
- Or does it take just 10 doing intensive data entry and queries?
- What is the probability of that limiting situation occurring? Is that acceptable?

Testing is also the art of assessing the application's quality. Quality is a vague term and can mean different things for each person, especially for the IT team member and the end-user. When quality is clearly defined, documented, and understood by all team members, quality is not subjective; it is part of a defined system. It is essential that the project manager, the end-user team, and the project team have a solid understanding of what quality means for this project. This directly relates back to the application's priorities that were discussed in *Chapter 8: Knowing the End-Result*. The application priorities are those factors that guide the project manager in making trade-offs between scope, schedule, and budget. They are the factors that determine if the application is a quality one. During testing, the specific application priorities really drive the rate of testing and repair. The priorities help to determine if testing and repair is done and the application is ready to implement. For example, if it was determined that accuracy is critical, then testing will continue until the accuracy of the application is acceptable. If, however, the schedule is more important, then testing will continue only for the allotted period of time. Other application priorities, such as usability, performance, and availability, will determine which problems are repaired before others.

Overall, testing is successful when it:

- Begins at the right time
- Employs various testing types and techniques
- Is prepared for effectively

Timing

The point at which testing should start is illustrated in Figure 12–1. Like construction, testing begins early in this process; it does not wait for the completion of design. In fact, testing begins before construction. What is being tested? Designs and prototypes are undergoing a specific type of testing called "usability testing." Usability testing is the process of verifying that the navigational flow and overall user interface decisions are acceptable to and understandable by the end-user. Usability testing verifies that the principles of effective design have been applied in an appropriate manner. Usability testing is essential for any application with a GUI.

With client/server applications, testing must start as soon in the process as possible. There are more risks associated with client/server applications and testing is a form of risk management. There are also more stages and types of testing to be completed, so more time must be allotted to the overall testing process.

Stages and Types

Testing, when done correctly, employs multiple testing techniques. The application is being tested at various levels for different types of potential problems. Testing, like the rest of the client/server development process, does not follow a linear process. In fact, many times, project teams "under-test" because they conduct testing in a linear fashion. Testing must be conducted in an iterative manner. Figure 12–2 illustrates the multi-tiered iterative testing technique.

As the figure shows, there are five stages of testing (component, string, functional group, system, and operations), which use eight testing types (compliance, usability, performance, stress, standard tasks, exceptions, acceptance, and regression).

The testing stages are represented by the horizontal bars. A test stage is defined by the number of application components that are being tested. Initially, one component is being tested, such as a single server program or a single window. The number of components are increased until, finally, the entire application is tested by running the application under realistic production conditions.

Testing stages also differ in the breadth of the application. Initially, testing is conducted at a very narrow application

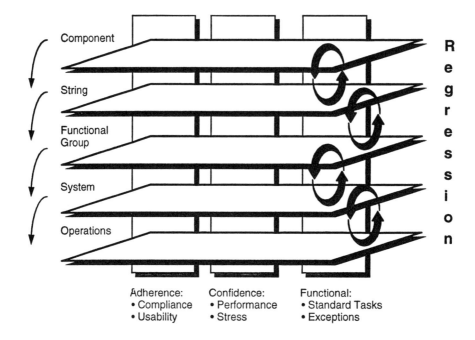

FIGURE 12-2. The multi-tiered testing technique.

breadth: the component. Problems are being sought in individual modules. Report layouts are being verified. Single window interaction is being tested. Once the various types of testing are completed at the component level, the breadth increases. Testing is done at the string level and answers the following questions:

■ Does program A pass the necessary information to program B?

■ Do the various windows that make up one module work together well?

■ Does window management work properly?

■ Does the client module call the server module?

■ Does the server module provide the correct response?

When the strings are stable and have been tested sufficiently, the functional groups are tested. The functional groups consist of the front to back processes that are needed to complete a set of similar functions. This stage of testing requires very detailed test plans and scenarios. Functional group testing answers the following questions:

- Is the information entered at the window processed correctly through the application?
- Does it appear correctly on the database? On reports?
- Do the corresponding functions utilize the information properly?

Once the functional groups have been tested, they are combined and the entire system is tested. Many times, data problems are discovered during this stage of testing. Data elements were defined consistently by each functional group, but the definitions were not consistent across groups. The following questions are answered during this type of testing:

- Does it work from front to back?
- Do the functional groups work together?
- Do they pass the necessary information back and forth, and process it correctly?
- Are all the various functions working together as necessary?

The final stage of testing is operations testing. This stage increases the breadth of testing to include all the systems, database, and network operations necessary to run the application in a true production environment. During system testing, tests are still run in a pseudo-production environment, with significant interference from the testing teams. During operations testing, the tests occur in as real a production environment as possible, with little to no interference. The complete application is tested during this final stage.

In Figure 12–2, the eight testing types are represented by the vertical bars. A test type is defined by the objective, or focus, of the testing. Six of the testing types are grouped into three categories: adherence, confidence, and functional. Acceptance testing and regression testing are also testing types. The type of testing refers to what portion of the application is being tested, and for what. For example, the testing types of usability and compliance are focused on verifying adherence to specific standards. The confidence testing types focus on proving the confidence placed in the application, specifically in its performance and ability to handle stress. Each test type is further defined in Table 12–1.

During testing, it is important that all completed components of the application go through all types and stages of testing. This ensures that the application is thoroughly tested and ready for "industrial-strength" use. The level of intensity applied to each type of testing during each stage, however, does not remain constant. During component and string testing, more effort is expended on compliance and usability testing than on performance and stress testing. During system and operations testing, testing is more focused on standard tasks and exception processing than on compliance and usability because those areas have already been thoroughly tested and stabilized.

Preparing for Successful Testing

The multi-tiered iterative testing process can only be successful if sufficient preparation has been done. The testing teams must know what to test and when. They must also have a good understanding of the application components and their corresponding functions. It is important to begin preparing for testing during design. Unfortunately, many projects do not start test preparation until the start of the testing process and then are not adequately prepared.

Testing benefits greatly when test scenarios and test plans are developed by the application's designers, as well as by the

TABLE 12–1. TESTING TYPES

Type	Objectives
Compliance	■ Verify that the application components comply with various standards, such as GUI design, naming, and coding standards ■ Identify non-standard uses of data elements, called procedures, error routines, etc. ■ Completed by usability tester, technical tester
Usability	■ Verify that the user interface components (GUI, documentation, training, help) are clear, consistent, usable, and follow principles of effective design ■ Test the behavior of the user interface components ■ Completed by usability tester
Performance	■ Test the technical performance of the application under various, realistic scenarios ■ Completed by technical tester
Stress	■ Test the application's response to various stressors, such as high volumes, "garbage" data, high traffic, minimum & maximum values, etc. ■ Identify the limits and points at which the application breaks down and how it responds to worst-case scenarios ■ Completed by functional tester, usability tester, technical tester
Standard Tasks	■ Test the functionality of the application components, focusing on the standard tasks that are performed in the user task flows and the corresponding business rules ■ Completed by functional tester
Exception Processing	■ Test the functionality of the application components, focusing on the non-standard and exception processing tasks that are performed in the user task flows ■ Completed by functional tester
Acceptance	■ Verify that the application is sufficiently stable and tested and is ready to move to the next stage of testing ■ Completed by functional tester, usability tester, technical tester
Regression	■ Verify that changes/repairs to components did not adversely affect the application ■ Completed by functional tester, usability tester, technical tester

end-users. When the designer creates the test deliverables, the testing team does not need to have as much detailed functional knowledge. More importantly, the designer is closer to the initial description of the functionality; there is less chance of misinterpreting the end-user's needs.

Many of the design documents can double as testing input documents, such as the task analysis, the Control-Action-Response Diagram, and the window and report layouts. The design documents also describe the business rules that must be tested at each stage. There are several key deliverables that are used during the testing process; they are described in Table 12–2.

TABLE **12–2.**   KEY TESTING DELIVERABLES

Deliverable	Description
Test Conditions	■ Description of the detailed items to be tested ■ May be documented in a test matrix: cross-references the test condition with the test scenarios in which it is tested, to the test data that is used to create the condition
Test Scenario	■ Group of test conditions that are combined based on common functionality to be tested ■ Is accompanied by a test plan (script or approach for testing; based on task analysis deliverables) ■ May be categorized or combined into larger scenarios, commonly called test cases
Test Data	■ Reference to specific input record, data to be entered, or database values that must exist ■ May be documented in a test matrix: cross-references the test condition with the test scenarios in which it is tested, to the test data that is used to create the condition
Expected Results	■ Description of the expected result of the test scenario using specific test data ■ Documented level of detail depends on the extent of the functional knowledge of the tester and the complexity of the test scenario

Testing is not an expense, a luxury, or an option. It is a requirement. A client/server project that sacrifices effective, integrated testing throughout the development lifecycle for meeting a project schedule will cost more and take longer to deliver. Client/server development projects require a disciplined commitment to quality if the failure rates are to be reduced.

IMPLEMENTATION

Implementation is the process of putting into practical effect the completed application. It involves all the work necessary to prepare the end-users, the production environment, the support team, the operations team, and the maintenance team to accept and effectively use the application. Many people think only of the conversion effort, or the process of "turning on" the new application and "shutting off" the old one. To be successful with client/server today, the project manager must consider implementation to include more than just conversion. Client/server projects will fail if the project team does not complete all the tasks required to fully implement the application. In the case of some applications, the implementation effort may exceed that of the development effort.

To be successful with implementation, the process must start at the right time and utilize the appropriate techniques. These are the same success factors discussed for construction and testing. Most important to success, however, is understanding what tasks are involved in a client/server implementation.

Client/server implementation consists of the following key tasks:

- Preparing the user communities
- Obtaining user acceptance
- Rolling-out the application

As Figure 12–1 illustrates, the implementation tasks should start during testing. Some preparation can start sooner, but the effort is greatly increased towards the end of testing, when a stable application is available.

As the client/server effort moves closer to implementation, the pressure builds to compromise the application to meet the project schedule. These compromises may be in feature sets, speed, future adaptability, functionality deemed non-critical, and most likely, quality assurance. If compromises must be made, be sure that the end-user is involved in the decision-making process. The end-user's level of involvement cannot be minimized or eliminated as implementation nears. Many times, the project team feels that they can make the best decision for the end-user. "If we let the end-user know about this issue, they'll want it fixed and we'll never end the project." That is not an attitude for success, and the project manager must ensure it does not flourish or get rewarded. Ultimately, the success of the project will be directly linked to the project manager's recognition of the end-user's role throughout the project lifecycle.

Preparing the User Communities

The users of an application are more than the business end-users who have been involved in the development effort. For an application to be successful, the project team must consider all the user communities:

■ Business end-users
■ Support (help desk) personnel
■ Operations personnel
■ Maintenance personnel

The project team must prepare all these different people as part of the implementation effort. No longer can you just turn over the application to the end-users, maintenance, support, and operations teams with a few days training and a binder or two. All these people must be adequately trained and accustomed to the application before the project team can step aside. The needs of each group differ, as well. Each group requires specific training, hands-on exposure, and documentation.

During the project scoping effort, it is essential to determine the approaches that will be used to prepare the maintenance, support, and operations teams.

- Will the development team become the support and maintenance teams? All of them, or just some? Who? How will they be cross-trained?

- Will people from the operations, support, and maintenance areas be part of the project team? At what point? In which roles?

- Will we develop training for these groups? What style? How much? Who will deliver it? When? How?

- How will documentation be developed? How much? How will it be distributed? Who will maintain it? How will we ensure that it is being kept current during the heat of development and testing?

Preparation of support, maintenance, and operations personnel should be started no later than the start of system testing. If the application is complex or very large, preparation should take place sooner. Ideally, the support team is involved in the design stage. They have a good perspective on what types of questions the end-users will have, or the common mistakes they make. Also, the support team speaks the "same language" as the development team and can provide valuable insight on how the end-users will use the application.

The approaches for preparing the business end-user must also be determined during the project scoping effort. Many times, client/server applications bring about a level of business process change (a.k.a., "re-engineering"). When there is business process change, there is also change management. Change management is the process of transitioning organizations to new structures, roles, processes, and rules. The scope of change management must be determined during the overall project scoping effort. Change management, when done well, requires very specific skills and a specific amount of time. These skill and time requirements must be considered during the project budgeting and scheduling process.

Regardless of the amount of business process change, any new application requires some training and documentation. The amount and style of training and documentation is determined during requirements-gathering. It is defined during the design stage and built during construction. Training and documentation will undergo a pilot, or testing, process with a subset of the business end-users. When the significant changes are made to the materials, they are then given to the larger set of end-users involved in the various stages of testing. Finally, when testing is almost over and the materials are in final format, the remaining members of the business end-user community are trained.

Remember that the business end-users and the operations personnel will be involved with testing, and must be prepared prior to its start. While testing will provide them with the necessary hands-on exposure, the actual training sessions and distribution of documentation must take place prior to the start of testing. If not, it is difficult to gauge whether testing problems are due to user error or if they are due to real problems in the application.

Obtaining User Acceptance

Just as the full community of users must be prepared, their acceptance must be obtained. User acceptance means that the users are "ready and able" to accept the application for use. They are satisfied with its overall quality: functionality, stability, performance, training, and documentation. They are satisfied with their level of preparation: they feel qualified to use, support, maintain, and operate the application. In other words, they are ready and the application is ready.

User acceptance is a formal process that requires management approval. It occurs after all stages of testing are completed and should use a formal sign-off document. Many times, the necessary people are part of a steering committee or group that sponsored the project; all people required for acceptance should be identified early in the project.

Contrary to popular belief, there is no hierarchy of acceptance. No one group's acceptance is more important than the others. It doesn't matter who pays for the application; if any one group does not feel they or the application is ready, then the application and corresponding development project usually fails. If the operations team cannot run the application, then what good is it that the business end-users are ready? If the business end-users are not satisfied with the functionality, then why does it matter that the support team is ready?

Rolling-out the Application

When the user community is prepared and has declared their acceptance of the application, it is ready to be rolled-out, or distributed for use. Prior to roll-out, the production environment requirements have been gathered and the environment designed, constructed, and tested. The roll-out process involves all the tasks necessary to establish and test the production environment for all the end-users, and the tasks necessary to distribute the application to bring it "on-line."

Roll-out can follow several approaches. At one end of the spectrum is the "big-bang" approach. In this approach, all the end-users are brought onto the new application at once; the old application, if one existed, is shut down. At the other end of the spectrum is the "phased" approach. In this approach, one area or group of end-users is brought on at a time; the existing application is shut down only when all end-users are using the new application. In the middle is the "parallel" approach in which some end-users use the new application and some use the old, gradually "weaning" the organization off the old application. Each approach has its own advantages and disadvantages. The approach must be selected during the requirements-gathering and project scoping efforts and be accepted by the end-user community.

The project roll-out must ensure that an effective transition occurs for the system's trainers and the business community's primary owner. The training group must focus on empowering the business end-users to take ownership of the application. Training materials, documentation, user guides, and on-line help must be complete, comprehensive, and understandable. Deployment technology must be in place prior to implementation training.

Implementation of each future release of an application should become easier and more transparent to the end-users. The nature of client/server development is to expect that the development cycle never ends and new releases will be delivered once or twice per annual cycle.

SUMMARY

Construction, testing, and implementation are the final stages of the development cycle, and they are just as critical as the earlier stages. The factors that contribute most to project success during these stages include:

- Beginning at the most effective and efficient time
- Employing the appropriate techniques for each stage

Construction is the process of creating tangible, concrete representations of the application. For construction to be successful, it must:

■ Begin at the appropriate time

■ Utilize tools, re-use, and standards

■ Consider unit testing part of the scope

Testing is the process of verifying the application from many different angles. Testing requires an iterative, multi-tiered technique that involves multiple stages and testing types. It cannot be compromised—minimizing testing will not save the project time or expense. Testing is successful when it:

■ Begins at the right time

■ Employs various testing types and techniques

■ Is effectively prepared for

Implementation is the process of making the application available for use in the final production environment. Client/server implementation consists of the following key tasks:

■ Preparing the user communities

■ Obtaining user acceptance

■ Rolling-out the application

When these stages are completed successfully, the project team has truly "put it all together!"

CHAPTER 13

CREATING THE ARCHITECTURE

Architecture:
Orderly arrangement of parts; structure

Quality client/server applications systems require a consistent foundation. The architecture must be well defined and it must establish a technical vision for everyone participating in the development effort. An architecture plan, like that provided to construct a building, is the blueprint for moving the application forward. A building architect's plan clearly conveys the vision of construction; the technical architect must create the same vision for the construction of the application. Unfortunately, the requirements of a client/server application are not as concrete as those of a building.

The technical architecture is essential both to project success and enterprise-wide system efforts. Although each development effort varies in functional focus, client/server efforts must follow a consistent and repetitive architecture strategy. The architecture must be clearly described to all project members; it provides a view of the application's technology, how it influences development, and how it addresses the demands of the business. A well-defined architecture blueprint provides all projects with a common and strong foundation. This foundation contributes to project success, resource leveraging, and cost containment.

This book has focused primarily on the business aspects of application development. Strategies for building software must recognize the importance of an underlying, clear architecture vision. The issues of best practices, tiered architectures, and strategies for re-use are common threads that client/server project managers face.

This chapter discusses the concerns of the client/server architecture:

- Creating an architecture strategy
- Structuring the architecture
- Following the architecture development cycle

CREATING AN ARCHITECTURE STRATEGY

As discussed in *Chapter 3: Preparing for Overall Success*, the Chief Information Officer (CIO) is responsible for creating the overall technology strategy. This strategy addresses the deployment environments, and to some extent, the development environments. The project manager uses this enterprise-wide strategy to develop the architecture strategy for the specific client/server application. The application-specific architecture strategy will be more detailed than the overall strategy. It will describe how specific technologies will be used to meet specific business needs.

A clear architecture strategy is critical to the success of a client/server project—the client/server architecture impacts many aspects of the client/server project. All people on the project must understand how decisions about the architecture impact their tasks. It is critical that a consistent strategy is created during project-scoping to define the architecture. This strategy will then be used to develop the application's architecture.

Specifically, the architecture strategy must address:

- Components of the architecture
- Technology dynamics
- Risk levels

Components of the Architecture

The traditional view of an architecture strategy was a simple statement that defined the tools, hardware, software, and standards. This high-level statement was sufficient in a development world where projects lasted more than two years, involved more than 40 technical resources, and business managers who knew better than to ask for revisions. Changes to any components of the architecture could be incorporated into the application without significant impact. Technologies were stable, project teams were experienced, and projects were lengthy.

The components of a client/server architecture still include tools, hardware, software, and standards. In fact, the architecture is the application's deployment environment, plus the project team's development environment. Refer to Figure 13–1 for a list of the various components of the architecture.

Primarily, the architecture strategy must clearly define the components of the architecture:

■ Client hardware and software configurations

■ Client and server operating and network operating platforms

■ Server and multi-server configurations

■ Network bandwidth and topology

Client Platform: Hardware, operating system software
Presentation Services: Window management, printing, multimedia software & hardware
Application Software: Executable code, business logic
Network: Hardware & software (operating, communications, support)
Middleware: Application communication & distribution software
Server Platform: Hardware, operating system software
Database: DBMS, data management software

FIGURE 13–1. Architecture components.

■ Processing speed demands

■ Capacity loads

■ Communication requirements

■ Tools and standards used to build and manage the architecture

The strategy must also describe how the application's architecture will differ from the configurations established in the overall technology strategy. The architecture strategy also describes how the various components will be linked together, what assumptions are being made, and how exceptions will be addressed.

The architecture strategy should also describe how an analysis of the ideal system components will be contrasted with existing or budgetary constrained components. It is better to recognize limitations on the front-end than overlook a system constraint that will have a severe impact on the project down the road.

Technology Dynamics

In addition to defining the components of the architecture, the architecture strategy must provide guidelines on creating flexible technology solutions. Business today is a changing, dynamic, evolving organism that must respond to competitive forces that arise without warning. Rapidly adaptable technology solutions help business respond to changing dynamics. Systems architected without flexibility will have a short life span, as will the careers of the managers who conjured up the architecture. Systems that fail to recognize the diverse operating and hardware platforms that will be deployed within the environment will have limited acceptance.

For example, the strategy must take into account the fact that applications, data, and technology may reside anywhere and everywhere. Today's architecture must support segmentation, distribution, and synchronization of complex information models, such as those in a sales force automation system.

Risk Levels

Many times the business risk level of an application is not considered when designing its architecture. This is the equivalent of designing a building on an earthquake fault without recognizing the potential disaster. The relative importance of a business system to the wealth, health, and future of an organization must be clearly assessed. The criticality of the application will influence the risk margins that can be applied to the architecture. The more central to the core of a business, the less willing an architect should be to apply bleeding-edge technology to the architecture. The architecture planning for a mission-critical application obviously demands far more analysis and adherence to internally developed standards than an ad-hoc, departmental project. The architecture strategy must define the levels of business risk and how they impact the architecture.

We frequently find mid-sized corporations in a position where their core technology was developed by a zealous technocrat who adapted bleeding-edge tools. As time passes, these tools frequently become minority players in the technical tool box. In addition to selecting architectural standards best on feature sets, it is critical to look at the market position and business viability of the technology provider. Long-term success is based on adopting a vision of where the path of technology is moving and where information systems must be positioned.

Other Considerations

The architecture strategy must also address:

- GUI requirements

  The ability of a business end-user to navigate within an application based on personal style rather than application control is a primary premise of the GUI architecture. End-users in environments where all applications are designed using a suite of standards are quick to adapt and use technology with a consistently reduced investment in training. The GUI places significant demands on the architectural vision of every project because it must be designed to support each type of dialog box and control button. The strategy must include the standards that will be used for the project and any limitations the architecture will place on the GUI.

■ Database requirements

The foundation of most legacy systems is a data-centric environment that focused on the data model as the primary foundation, around which the application was constructed. The client/server application is driven by functional prototypes that uncover underlying data entities. The architecture strategy must address how the database architect will keep the unfolding data structure in synch.

The wide distribution of hardware to desktops, remote offices, and foreign shores also has architectural impacts that add significant complexity to client/server architecture. As the distance and distribution of data evolves, driven by business demands, the pipelines that deliver and transmit information will be placed under constant stress. The architecture strategy must provide the capability to account for these dynamics.

■ Reusability strategies

A development team's commitment to the re-use of frequently used objects requires a long-term investment to obtain measurable returns. An effectively developed plan to manage and control objects has the potential to reduce development cycles significantly. From a strategic standpoint, understand that all projects now have some dependency to share or contribute objects to the object pool. This is a complex issue that requires company-wide standards for development tools, cross-project communications, and maintenance infrastructures. For example, if a company decides that it is committed to tracking postal zip codes in 5+4 fashion and all systems currently store and display only five zip code digits, how easy or difficult will this change be for the development resources? The architecture strategy must address how to assess the impact of an object change in one application across systems.

■ Integration requirements

The architecture strategy must address the concept of architectural integration with deployed client/server systems. As new applications are successfully deployed, business needs and levels of confidence will drive the demand to integrate legacy technology. New applications challenge the development team to build systems that move forward with compatibility and system openness. Integration demands a clear analysis of legacy dependencies, middleware capabilities, application program interfaces, and database capacities. The architecture strategy must bring together systems built by historical and unfamiliar resources. The complexity of remodeling an old home, the uncovering of unexpected structural weaknesses, is significantly more risky than new construction.

STRUCTURING THE ARCHITECTURE

Client/server technology should be highly scaleable. Leading technology tools are designed to address a desktop (or client) solution—a client attached to a network server, a client attached to a server with access to a mid-range or mainframe database, and a client connected through the Internet to a server anywhere on the planet. This requires the architecture to be structured effectively. Structuring the application consists of defining the number of architecture tiers and the number of application layers.

Architecture Tiers

A client/server application can be designed for implementation across one, many, or a combination of tiers. A tier refers to a physical level within a client/server system. For example, a customer service application used on a laptop by a field representative would be implemented using just one tier. All processing is completed on one physical machine. The same application can be implemented at the department level using client machines connected to a server—a two-tiered architecture.

Table 13–1 represents a simplistic view of client/server architecture tiers. In reality, there are many more combinations that can be implemented.

A client/server developer must have a clear understanding of the tiered architecture that drives the application's hardware and software. With each succeeding level, the architectural complexity expands significantly. The "Simplest Level" is a local client/server implementation, architected within a single PC. The "Full Implementation" is an architectural environment that forces Information Technology (IT) to support a world wide multi-platform solution.

Each tier outlined in Table 13–1 requires a different architecture strategy. A one-tiered, or simplest level, architecture supports initial prototyping and system development that is focused on desktop capability such as Microsoft's OLE. The migration of any application from one hardware tier to the next significantly impacts the complexity of the architecture. Each

TABLE 13–1.   CLIENT/SERVER TIERS

Platform Tiers	Client	Server	Host	Web
Simplest Level	Yes	No	No	No
2nd Level	Yes	Yes	No	No
3rd Level	Yes	Yes	Yes	No
Full Implementation	Yes	Yes	Yes	Yes

tier requires additional architecture components, which in turn increases the development effort.

Application Layers

Another way of structuring the application is through the definition of application layers, or partitions. Layering the application refers to how the application is structured. Ideally, the functional components are grouped and isolated from the technical components; this minimizes the impact of technology changes. It is a conceptual, platform-independent structuring of the application. The application layering approach is part of the application's architecture—it is part of the overall framework and places constraints on the development team.

Various texts address the technology behind the development layers of a client/server architecture. Each of these layers requires a different development strategy, specific tools, management approaches, and quality testing. The four basic layers of a client/server application are:

- Presentation
- Application Logic
- Business Rules
- Database

The presentation layer is the user interface (UI) view. This is the perspective most visible to the end-user community. Presentation style should be a combination of response to the end-user needs, application of UI industry standards, and internally established architectural standards.

The application logic is where the end-user's business process requirements meet the limits and challenges of technology tools. The logic of a procedural language, an event-driven solution, an object-oriented solution, or a meta-driven development tool must deliver information to back-end databases in a logical, efficient, and effective manner.

The implementation and maintenance of business rules are major leverage points for a highly successful client/server application. If the architectural choices support an independent layer for business rules, many of the hopes of a client/server project can be realized today and into the future.

The growth and success of client/server technology is driven by the success and enhanced feature sets provided within relational database engines. Access to the database must be secure, logical, and rapid and most importantly open to each of the layers described previously. The development tool sets will determine the positioning of the business rules relative to the application layer. The technical platform and database features will also determine options related to the development of SQL stored procedures and database triggers.

Relationship between Tiers and Layers

Once the technical architects have identified the number of architecture tiers and application layers, they must determine where each layer of the application will reside. This process may modify either the number of tiers selected or the defined layers.

When a single-tiered architecture is used, all layers of the application will reside on the client machine. This is obviously the simplest case. As the number of tiers increase, so does the complexity in deciding where layers will reside. Typically, the presentation layer resides on the client. The database layer (except for decodes tables and frequently accessed data) resides on the highest tier, generally a server or host machine. Some data, such as decodes and frequently access data, may reside on the client machine. The application logic layer and business rules layer can reside on the client or any other tier. The decision as to where those layers reside is influenced by:

- Performance requirements
- Maintainability issues

■ Complexity

■ Project team expertise

The technical architect must create guidelines for the rest of the project team, which describes how the application should be layered and what constraints are placed on the design.

THE ARCHITECTURE DEVELOPMENT CYCLE

Previous chapters have described the best development process for building client/server applications. They have intentionally not addressed the development of the architecture. It is important to understand the basic process, key decisions made at each point, and the flow of information between each stage. This same basic process is used for the development of the architecture. However, the architecture development cycle must occur ahead of the development of the rest of the application. Remember that the architecture places constraints on the design of the user interface, business processes, and database. Therefore, major portions of the architecture must be designed, prototyped, constructed, and tested prior to the design of the most critical functional groups. Figure 13–2 illustrates the evolution of the architecture as the business needs are refined and evolved.

The development cycle illustrated in Figure 13–2 clearly operates on two concurrent levels: the business requirements flow and the technology platform evolution. It is important to the success of a client/server development effort that development is iterative, and not linear. Just as there is iteration between deliverables of the various business requirements, there is iteration between architecture deliverables and business requirements deliverables.

The iterative nature of client/server development constantly requires responsible parties to determine if the technical architecture is in balance with the evolving business prototypes. Underlying the development flow, portrayed in Figure 13–2, is an ongoing refinement of design prototypes and busi-

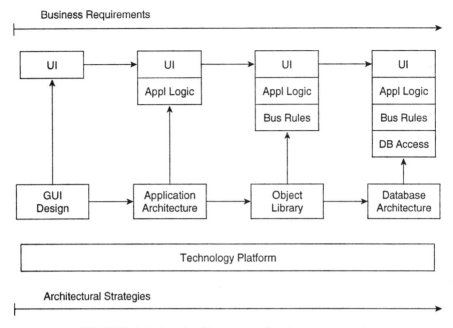

FIGURE 13–2. Architecture development cycle.

ness requirements. This, in turn, impacts the core of the under-lying technical foundation. This is an evolving effort, and it leaves much room for the project to spin out of control.

The project manager must have a clear understanding of the relationship between the development of the architecture and the rest of the application. This relationship must be re-flected in project plans, staffing, and priorities.

Gathering Technical Requirements

Gathering technical requirements is done by the technical ar-chitect and analysts. They are focused on understanding the re-quirements of the architecture—what the architecture must do for the rest of the application. For example, they are gathering performance requirements (speeds, response times, transaction rates, and sizes) and load requirements (number of end-users, maximum usage times, and "up-time" needs).

They gather these requirements from end-users, other technical architects, and industry experts. Many of the techniques discussed in *Chapter 9: Defining the Details* are appropriate for gathering technical requirements.

Analyzing and Designing the Architecture

The analysis of the architecture requirements must be based on business priorities. During analysis and design, consider the following issues:

- Change impact—What are the driving business issues that impact this application? How often will the features and demands that surround this application be driven to change? The more dynamic the environment, the more critical it is for the architecture to depend on components and technology that can adapt to change. Business environments that are based on supporting accounting needs are seldom dynamic in functional change. Solutions that support sales and marketing must be dynamic to respond to changing business conditions.

- Existing tool sets—What is the investment in the existing architecture and accompanying tools? What is the future of the in-place tool sets? Are there growth or capacity limits? Is maintenance of the architecture a challenge? Are the current tools maintainable? How far are they from the current release supported by the vendor? Are these tools compatible with an open system environment?

- Integration—With what other systems must this application interface? Can changes be made to the interfaced systems? Where do these systems reside? Who owns the integration? What are the timing issues that these system create?

- Reusability—What commitment does the development team have to manage and create business objects? Are there object repositories in place to check in and out objects?

■ Modularity—How much functionality will be contained in each module? How will the impact of changes in functionality be minimized? Should each module perform only one function? How does this fit with the reusability strategy?

Constructing and Testing the Architecture

Building and testing the architecture is completed by technical programmers and testers. They follow the same processes and use the same techniques as those described in *Chapter 12: Putting It All Together*. In addition, this part of the development process includes:

■ Integration plans
■ Code optimizing
■ Database tuning
■ Code packaging procedures

SUMMARY

In order to build a quality client/server application, there must be a solid foundation. The architecture must provide the foundation for the rest of the application. The architecture will be well-defined and built if the project team effectively:

■ Creates an architecture strategy;
■ Structures the architecture; and
■ Follows the architecture development cycle.

Most importantly, the team must remember that the architecture is no longer focused purely on the technology. It must be aligned with the demands and directions of the business world.

PART 4

FUTURE DIRECTIONS AND CHALLENGES

CHAPTER 14

WHAT COMES NEXT?

Future:
A prospective or expected condition, especially one considered with regard to growth, advancement, or development

Our crystal ball is no clearer than that of the next technology expert. We recognize that commercial software development tools are all in evolutionary states. But we also believe that core infrastructure, methods, standards, and quality processes will continue to remain basically as we have discussed in detail throughout this book.

When we began to write this book, the Internet, Java™, Active X™, and related technology were in the distant horizon, or more aptly, "in the fog" of client/server development. The Web development tools that we see swirling around corporate offices will continue to evolve and mature. This will not be the end of the technology evolution. The skillful technology manager must maintain a focus in the present and an eye on the future.

The complexity of project scope and diversity will continue to change in response to new technology. For example, as the pressures to build and integrate Internet and intranet applications increase, development projects will incorporate end-users that exist far outside the corporate structure.

As new tools are introduced to Information Technology (IT) development teams, they will not initially ship with the team-based infrastructure-support features that quality efforts require. This will demand that management supplement this technology with a mature organizational process that is reliable and repeatable. It will pressure development teams to integrate these new tools into the development process in a manageable form.

In a book written by Geoffrey Moore, *Inside the Tornado*, he makes the observation that pragmatists are the people most likely to be in charge of a company's mission-critical systems. They know this infrastructure is only marginally stable, and they are careful to protect it from novel intrusions. Mr. Moore is a technology marketing expert, but his statement clearly conveys the challenge that IT organizations throughout the world now face.

Throughout this book, we have expressed a clear message that IT must carefully align mission, vision, structure, and capability to respond to rapidly changing business conditions. These pressures are increasing exponentially as technology enables a new world marketplace. This global technology environment will test the strength and stability of every IT organization's infrastructure.

FUTURE TRENDS

Our development and management strategies support "client/ network-centric" projects as well as "client/server-oriented" efforts. The term "client/network" is an extension of client/ server, which recognizes that the end-user of the future will require access to information that is resident on any number of servers present anywhere within a network's global reach. The technology that integrates Web browsers and Web servers will force IT teams to tackle problems, such as language localization, in ways that most organizations have never needed to support.

Technology will drive opportunities to expand electronic commerce, which will still require the discipline and structure that industry standards, such as Electronic Data Interchange (EDI), have brought to supporting business applications. IT shops that have implemented an EDI architecture will be challenged to move their data pipelines from value-added networks to the Internet. The perception that the Information Super Highway is a "freeway" will drive EDI migration and electronic commerce project expansion. This global movement of data will create opportunities to expand and enhance IT infrastructure.

Pressures will continue to impact software development requirements, but they will not change the processes, methods, and disciplines required to develop, maintain, and deploy quality software. IT professionals will continue to adapt to the ever-changing technology pallet and demands for increased response to changing business conditions. The impact will manifest itself in terms of the "expansion of technology's sphere of influence" within every organization.

These changing dynamics will impact IT development teams in the following ways:

- Departmental systems will shift to enterprise solutions.
- Enterprise solutions will expand to integrate access by external entities.
- Web-enabled solutions will demand restructuring of business applications.
- Data Warehouse deployment and integration will continue to evolve.
- Global access to network servers will expand technical support demands and resource requirements.
- Rapidly adaptable technology will expand the role of business analysts in moving business applications closer to changing business processes.
- Integration of workflows and business processes into business applications will expand the application scope of new technology.

Each of these dynamics requires new strategies, modified teams, and new processes adapted to new technologies. At its core, the discipline of software development remains consistent despite the changes in the surrounding environment. The scope of projects, complexity of applications, and the proximity of the user community will change due to the above dynamics. As is often the perspective in a technical world, the "only constant is change."

The pendulum of technology development will continue to swing. In the past 30 to 40 years that the "science of software development" has been applied to business environments, we have seen a migration from highly centralized to a largely decentralized function. Today, we are beginning to swing back from decentralized teams to a hybrid. This hybrid will need to support rapid deployment of systems with centralized planning and coordination.

The complex nature of software serving diverse end-user communities will increasingly demand skilled managers and technicians. Development tools that are driven by meta-structures and enable software to change rapidly in an evolving business world will significantly impact the responsibilities and roles of IT professionals.

CONCLUSION

Many articles have been written discussing the levels of stress and job dissatisfaction experienced by software developers and related technologists. The work loads, stress levels, and demands placed on these skilled resources must be addressed. The excitement of, and opportunities given to, those who have made career commitments to software development must be maintained.

The tools will change. The end-user will be geographically dispersed. The technology will adapt to business processes faster. The demands for software will increase. What was a client/server application for a 25 user department will become a Web-enabled application for world-wide access.

Those of us who have destroyed source code, deleted critical files, or just gone home blurry-eyed long after everyone else has gone to sleep, know the pain and love that we feel toward building software applications. We know the pride that is taken in deploying a complete, user-accepted, functional system. We know the frustration and rationale that comes with canceled or failed projects.

This book was written as a commitment to those software developers who long for and deserve a manager who understands the right way to direct a software project. No matter how effective we have been at conveying a vision of structure, method, and approach within the pages of this book, we all must recognize that process and technology depend on quality people.

PART 5

APPENDIX

GLOSSARY

Analysis Act of breaking apart a list of requirements into its various smaller components

Application Technology solution to a business problem; system; collection of software programs

Application Framework Approach to layering and distribution for a client/server application

Application Priority Item that directly impacts the application's scope

Application Release Discrete set of new or improved functionality that provides specific benefits

Architecture Technical components that allow the application to interact with the deployment environment

Business Rule Underlying principle that drives business decisions; business rules are reflected in data attributes and relationships, process flows, and events

Business Specialist Individual responsible for providing input, review and feedback on business terminology and requirements

Change Management Process of transitioning organizations to new structures, roles, processes, and rules

Change Request Document that details a desired modification to an application

Client When used in the term "client/server," refers to the portion of the application that runs on a local machine, typically responsible for user interface and some business processing; this portion of the application may run on a personal computer or workstation

Client/Server Form of distributed computing in which completion of a transaction is divided across multiple physical machines, each used to the best of their capabilities

Component Portion of an application

Construction Process of creating tangible, concrete representations of the application

Custom Development Approach Process in which an application is built from new or slightly modified components

Database Architect Individual responsible for the design and development of the physical databases implemented

Deliverable End-result of a development task

Deployment Environment Technical environment in which an application will run (operating systems, communications, networks, databases, etc.)

Design Process of detailing, in a systematic manner, the specifics of the application

Development Approach The general process or style followed in developing an application; the main development approaches include: packaged-system, custom and maintenance

Development Environment All items needed for the development of an application: technical environment (operating systems, communications, networks, databases, etc.) and development aids (tools, techniques, and standards)

Development Process Collection of specific steps, deliverables and techniques that are used to build an application (also known as methodology)

Dialog Navigation Model Template for the entire user interface, consisting of the main menu bar with the corresponding menu options

Distributed Processing A form of computing in which the completion of a transaction requires multiple processors

End-User General term used to describe a member of the business community who will use an application

End-User Profile Deliverable that describes the types of people who will use the application

End-User Manager Individual responsible for obtaining, directing, and maintaining end-user involvement in the project

Executive Sponsor Individual responsible for providing overall high-level direction for the project

Functional Architect Individual responsible for defining the scope of the functional components of the application and ensuring that the application will solve the business problems presented

Functional Analyst Individual responsible for gathering and analyzing functional requirements

Functional Designer Individual responsible for translating models into designs for use by the interface and technical teams

Functional Group Major pieces of functionality represented by a set of windows, reports, and back-end processes that, when combined, provide a business function that has value to the end-users

Functional Programmer Individual responsible for developing code that provides the business functionality and reusable components of the application

Functional Tester Individual responsible for testing the business components of the application

Functional Testing Verifying that the application is providing the business functions as they are needed

High-Fidelity Prototype Fully interactive prototype with deep functionality

Implementation Process of putting into practical effect the completed application

Infrastructure Technical backbone of the organization that includes computer networks, desktop and departmental systems, communication systems (voicemail, e-mail), and telecommunications networks

Infrastructure Liaison Individual responsible for ensuring services are received from infrastructure group

Instructional Designer Individual responsible for designing and developing training materials

Interface Architect Individual responsible for designing the application's overall look-and-feel

Interface Designer Individual responsible for identifying and designing all windows of the application

Interface Programmer Individual responsible for developing code that provides the full graphical user interface and reusable components of the application

Internet World-wide collection of private networks interconnected through public links used to display, communicate, and maintain information

Intranet Private network of servers using internet-technology to display, communicate and maintain information

Joint Application Design Design technique in which the design team and the end-user team jointly design critical portions of the application

Joint Requirements Planning Requirements-gathering technique in which the development team and the end-user team jointly define and refine the application's requirements

Layer Grouping of application components that corresponds to a tier in an attempt to minimize the impact of changes

Legacy Business applications that are dependent on software development tools, hardware and/or operating environments that are no longer supported by the product's vendor

Low-Fidelity Prototype Paper-based or limited interaction prototype with limited functionality

Maintenance Approach Process in which an application, currently used in production, is modified or enhanced

Management Support Individual responsible for all support functions: project management tool administration and data entry, status report generation, data-gathering, etc.

Methodology Collection of specific steps, deliverables and techniques that are used to build an application

Modularity Packaging of code into small self-contained modules that provide limited functionality

Object Conceptual collection of data and associated processing that can be used to describe and build an application

Object-oriented Approach to developing systems that is based on use of the objects throughout design and construction

Package Selection & Implementation Approach Process in which an existing software package is modified and installed to meet specific business and technical requirements

Portfolio Planning Analyzing the overall list of project requests/initiatives, across teams and functional areas, and placing resources on the ones most critical to the business

Project Advisor Individual responsible for providing feedback and advice on concerns of the project manager; staffed by peer of project manager outside of project

Project Manager Individual responsible for providing day-to-day direction for the project

Prototyping Technique used during the design process that results in the development of better designs

Reusability Multiple use of components within one application, or from one application to another

Reusability Liaison Individual responsible for determining and managing the project's approach towards reusability

Role Collection of skills that have responsibility for completing specific tasks

Server When used in the term "client/server," refers to the portion of the application that runs on a remote machine, typically responsible for data access and business processing; this portion of the application may run on a network file server machine, mainframe, database server machine, or internet server machine

Team Leader Individual responsible for providing day-to-day direction for the team

Technical Analyst Individual responsible for gathering and analyzing technical requirements

Technical Architect Individual responsible for designing the application's architecture framework

Technical Designer Individual responsible for translating models into designs of the system architecture

Technical Programmer Individual responsible for developing code that provides the architecture functionality and reusable components

Technical Support Individual responsible for providing support and coordination for the development environment

Technical Tester   Individual responsible for testing the architecture components of the application

Technical Writer   Individual responsible for designing and developing hard-copy documentation and on-line help

Tier   Physical level within a client/server application's architecture

Trainer   Individual responsible for delivering training

Usability Tester   Individual responsible for testing all the interface components of the application

User Acceptance   Statement that all users are satisfied with their level of preparation and the quality of the application

Vendor Liaison   Individual responsible for coordinating all vendor activities

SUGGESTED READINGS

August, Judy. *Joint Application Design: The Group Session Approach to System Design*. Englewood Cliffs, NJ: Prentice Hall, 1991.

Bell, Chip, Ron Zemke. *Managing Knock Your Socks Off Service*. New York, NY: AMACOM, 1992.

Brooks Jr., Frederick. *The Mythical Man-Month: Essays on Software Engineering, Anniversary Edition*. Reading, MA: Addison-Wesley Publishing Company, 1995.

Jacobson, Ivar. *Object-Oriented Software Engineering*. Reading, MA: Addison-Wesley Publishing Company, 1992.

Lee, Geoff. *Object-Oriented GUI Application Development*. Englewood Cliffs, NJ: Prentice Hall, 1993.

Martin, James. *Rapid Application Development*. New York, NY: Macmillan Publishing Company, 1991.

Nielsen, Jakob. *Usability Engineering*. Cambridge, MA: Academics Press, 1993.

Orfali, Robert, Dan Harkey, Jeri Edwards. *The Essential Client/Server Survival Guide: Second Edition*. John Wiley & Sons, 1996.

Taylor, David. *Object-Oriented Technology: A Manager's Guide*. Reading, MA: Addison-Wesley Publishing Company, 1990.

Wirfs-Brock, Rebecca, Brian Wilkerson, Lauren Wiener. *Designing Object-Oriented Software.* Englewood Cliffs, NJ: Prentice Hall, 1990.

Vaskevitch, David. *Client/Server Strategies: A Survival Guide for Corporate Reengineers.* San Mateo, CA: IDG Books Worldwide, 1993.

INDEX

MCP.com (book)
Client/Server Computing

NOS   points foils

Unix — Security
NT   — Application Sharing
Novell — Services

Client Needs —▷ | client | MIDDLE WARE | SERVER |

WINDOWS CE

OPTIMIZE $ IDEAL PERFORMANCE FOR LOWEST COST

data Mining indeed books
SAP —> RDBMS   fortune 500 company
    SAP. R3